A NewsHound's Guide to Student Journalism

A NEWS HOUND'S
GUIDE TO STUDENT JOURNALISM

Katina Paron, MJE, & Javier Güelfi

ISBN (print) 978-1-4766-7591-6
ISBN (ebook) 978-1-4766-3440-1

LIBRARY OF CONGRESS CATALOGUING DATA ARE AVAILABLE

BRITISH LIBRARY CATALOGUING DATA ARE AVAILABLE

Printed in the United States of America

*McFarland & Company, Inc., Publishers
Box 611, Jefferson, North Carolina 28640
www.mcfarlandpub.com*

To my love, my life, my Will.
Thank you for picking me out of everyone.
—Katina

A Mariana, la luz de nuestro amor ilumina mi camino.
—Javier

Find your voice. Do what it takes. Make sure you make lots of mistakes.
—Dar Williams, "Teenagers, Kick Our Butts," *End of the Summer*

Table of Contents

Acknowledgments

A big THANK YOU to all of those who helped us create this book: Indrani Sen, Trixie's godmother; Amanda Prost, our wordsmithing confidante; Shannon Berning and Jane Isay for talking us off ledges and helping us navigate unfamiliar territory; Linda Shockley at Dow Jones News Fund for getting "NewsHounds" from the get go; To the brilliant insight of our reviewers and content consultants: Carl Bialik, Tom Gayda, Cathy Kaczmarek, Eileen Markey, Frank LoMonte, Steve O'Donoghue, and Polly Schoenfeld; James Fergusson, our amazing copyeditor; the JAWdesses for their encouragement and smarts; the JEA listserv for classroom heroics and constant inspiration; the NYC journalism educator community for their gratitude and colleagueship; Tim Harper for latching on early and letting go gracefully; Jere Hester for being the nicest guy in the biz; Charlotte Cooper, for her brilliance, guidance, and networking pizzaz; To all the teens who let Katina edit and teach them; And, of course, to Will Turnage and Mariana Marcaletti for putting up with us.

This book exists because these individuals believe in young people's capacity to do great things. Thank you.

Sharon K. D´Agostino; The Dow Jones News Fund; Linda Bowen; Nancy Schuh; Indrani Sen; Catherine Fruchey; Tim Harper; Ramit Kreitner; Amanda Prost; Professor Geanne Belton; W.J. Michael Clark; David Cruz; Wayne Dawkins; The Honorable Alice M. Dear; John J. Edwards III; Janine Feczko; Polly Flonder Schoenfeld; Nathan & Simone Gaffin; Patricia A. Gill; Alicia Glavin; Jessica Greenwood; Emelie Haigh; Vera Haller; Sanda Htyte; Tom Hutchinson; In honor of Margaret Turnage; In honor of Maria P. Paron; In honor of young muckrakers and their mentors; Kate Kennedy; Alice Lincoln; Elizabeth Mandel; Zachary Maxwell; John Mayo-Smith; Dean McRobie; Tzyh Ng; Nicola Nieburg; Jan Paschal; Julie Renwick; Rem Reynolds; Thalia Schunk; Alex Selkirk; Zane Selkirk; Sarah Smiley; Jennifer Sullam; Brian Sweeney; Rachel Swinnen; Molly Touger; Rob Wininger; Theresa Wozunk & Jere Hester; Reniqua Allen; Leslie Berger; Alex Berke; Juhie Bhatia; Carl Bialik; Myles Black Miller; S. M. Boghosian; Michael D. Bolden; Janna Braun; Jill Burns; Meagan L. Butler; Darron Foy; Christina Carrega; Adriana Chavira; Jean Cochran; Kyla Dippong; Petra Domingo and family; M. Tyler Dukes; Carla Echevarria; Kristen Elechko; Brian Eriksen; Ivana Espinet; Jeanmarie Evelly; James Fergusson; Julie Fischoff & Matt Franks; Rebekah L. Goode; Danielle Gould; Suzanne Grossman; Amanda Harding; Ida M. Hoffmann, CJE; Peter Hogness; Katie Honan; In honor of Dorothy Dostalek; In honor of Rich Cameron; In honor of Nick Ferentinos; Catherine Kaczmarek; Karen Mochizuki Kano; Bari Katz; Joel Kuszai; James Kutz & Lou Beltrami; Nomi Krim Edwards; Mike Lee; Nicole Lisa; Natalie Maneval; Mariana Marcaletti; Tim Maylander; Erin Meeker; M&M Mercurio; Mary H. Miller; NYNPA Education Services Director; Joshua Mills; Sol Mills; Chandler Miranda; Jordan Moss; Ann Neary; Michele Netto; Ilana Novick; Jennifer Owens Hill; Kazuo Ozawa; Paul Paron; Angeli Rasbury; Donna Rickles; Gabriela Rodriguez Beron; Jayna Marie Rust; Alan Salisbury; Tina Schoenherr; Adam

Schweigert; Roxanne L. Scott; Judy Shepherd-King; Kim Small; Thy Than; Adam Thompson; Amanda Thieroff; Naomi Touger; Tasha Turner; Inés & Bryan Vaniman; Linda Villarosa; Ben Abelson; Cynthia Almansi; Sean Berleman; Michael Bobelian; James Bourland; Richard Cameron; David Carl; Leonardo Castañeda; Paola Colombo; Ilsa Cowen; J. Ford; James G. Frierson; Jake Fritz; Zoe Gedeon; Samantha Georgi; Marie Louie Gilot; Chloe Gottlieb; Ed Gragert; In Honor of the Next Generation of Journalists Seeking Truth; Nicole Paron; Pearland Junior High; West Oleum Staff; David Peris; Joanne Parsont; Perrie Rizzo; Serena Schonbrun Connelly; Sarah Selig; Zack Seward; E. Donna Shepherd; Karl Sluis; Robyn Sperling; Sam Swope; Kathryn Tomajan; Jennifer Weiss; Amy White; and Daniel Zeiger

Special Thanks to

Bierce & Kenerson, P.C.; Law Offices of Lawrence B. Goodwin, PLLC; Annaliese Griffin; Betty Ming Liu; Mark Pennington; Sandya Viswanathan; and Savitha Viswanathan

> **Learn more about careers in journalism by visiting Dow Jones News Fund at https://dowjonesnewsfund.org/**

Verification

"The essence of journalism is a discipline of verification."—Bill Kovach and Tom Rosenstiel, *The Elements of Journalism*

Getting It Right Everytime

Hunches, gut feelings, educated guesses—reporters pride themselves on their keen instincts. We work hard to develop sources, and we make sure that we're the first to hear tips, rumors, or secrets. That's how a lot of great stories start. But no matter how great your instincts are, no matter how solid that tip is, you need a lot more than tips and instincts to write a news story.

Verification Is a Key Element of Journalism

Every fact in your story, every number, assertion, and quote needs to be checked to make sure it's accurate. We're all human, and we each come to every story with a set of pre-conceptions and prejudices, and those can shape our telling of a story. Since we can't be objective, we rely on a method that is objective.

The Verification Method

See it to believe it—The best facts are those you know firsthand or have seen with your own eyes.

Back up your facts—Any facts you didn't witness firsthand should be confirmed with three or more reliable sources who have first-hand knowledge/expertise.

Verify while you're reporting—Ask all of your interviewees to confirm the spelling of their name, as well as their age and grade or job description. Take detailed notes or record your interviews.

Research is important—Make sure all of your research sources are reliable. (No Wikipedia!)

Be transparent—Your reader should know where each piece of information came from. Cite the source, whether it's something you observed, researched, or learned from a reliable person.

Keep a reporting and research list—List the contact info of sources, books or papers you consulted, and online links. You should be able to follow your own reporting path.

Fact-check your work—Double and triple-check any numbers and your math and spelling. Check quotes to make sure they've been accurately transcribed from your notes. If any of the facts or pieces of the narrative don't make sense, go back for clarification.

Interviewing Tips

Be Human, Be Present, and Listen

Before you approach someone for an interview, make sure you prepare your questions—and yourself—in advance. Dress appropriately and act interested in what your source is saying. You should identify yourself as a reporter and indicate that you're writing an article for a newspaper or news site. As you conduct the interview, think about it as a conversation with a purpose. You want it to feel natural, but make sure you stay in control.

You're Not Done Yet!

Before you say goodbye to your interviewee: Look over your notes quickly and make sure you don't need more clarification on something.

Immediately following the interview: Read over your notes carefully and make sure you have everything you need. If you only wrote down half a quote, now is the time to complete it, when everything is fresh in your head.

Sources

Identifying Key Players

Sources are to journalists what ingredients are to chefs. You can't get cooking without them.

Before you start writing down your questions for an interview, you have to consider your subject. Questions for the principal about the prom dress code policy will be very different than the questions you ask students about the same policy.

The more sources of information you have, the better your article will be. How do you identify sources? Ask yourself:

- Who is directly impacted?
- Who are the decision makers?
- Who has personal experience with the topic?
- Who has professional experience with the topic?

Remember, in an article people's opinions are less meaningful than their experiences. Teens are the experts of their own experiences. Get them to talk about what they know best— themselves. Your goal is to get as close to the core of the story as you can and then branch out from there.

Keep in mind that students can be both directly impacted *and* the decision makers. If you are writing about a student council decision, you'll need to talk to those who made the decision (students) and those who are impacted by it (students). Try to avoid letting people talk on behalf of others; let people represent themselves.

Types of Sources

Not all sources are people and not all sources are equal. Sources can also refer to official documents, reference material and online research. You should make it a point to have a variety of sources for all of your stories. Here are two main categories of sources:

Primary Sources: People who were there, who witnessed or experienced the thing happening. Documents that provide proof (a video, an email, police report, etc.)

Secondary Sources: Documentation after the fact by people who weren't there: a professor who studies the topic, a documentary, a news report, etc. These may not be as reliable as primary souces, but do play an important role in your story.

It may seem like primary sources are the place to focus your energies, but there is something to be said for being a few steps away in order to see the bigger picture. In many stories, it is valuable to have an expert provide context and a wide angle view of the situation. This source is know as a **Voice of Authority**. Depending on the topic, the source might be a leader in the community, a researcher, a university professor, an author, or a school counselor. You want someone removed from the immediacy of who or what you are writing about, but they need to have professional experience in the topic.

To be a credible source of news information to your reader, you need to make sure your sources are trustworthy and reliable. Here are some questions that will help you determine that about a source:

- How does the source benefit from being quoted or having a specific perspective shared?
- How informed is the source on the issue at hand?
- How does the source know this information? Have they studied it? Are they trained to understand it?
- Can what the source said be verified through other means (public records, research studies, other experts, etc.)?
- Does the information the source provide help the reader understand the issue?

Control the Narrative

While sources are integral to your story, they do not have the right to control what you write. Some sources will only agree to interviews if they can see the questions in advance or review the article before publication. These actions are journalistic red flags. It's unethical to hand over the reins of your reporting because it destroys your credibility and independence as a journalist and sets a bad precedent for others.

Placate these sources by providing them a bulleted list of 3–5 topic areas your questions will cover and offer to read back the source's quotes that made it into the article. This is a great way to fact-check the information in your story. The source can't change the meaning of a quote or perfect the wording, but he or she can correct any outright errors.

Your sources may have varying levels of comfort with being quoted. Make sure you are both on the same page and that you understand these definitions:

On the record: You can publish what a source says and use his or her name.

On background: The reporter can use the information provided but can't identify the source by name. How the source is identified job title, connection to story's subject, should be negotiated with the source beforehand.

Deep background or Non-attributable: You can use the information, but you may not identify the source in any way.

Off the record: You can't publish the information or the name of the source.

Transparency in Sourcing:

Whenever possible you want to identify your sources fully. This creates trust and helps your readers follow the story better. But sometimes, people who are willing to be interviewed don't want their names published.

The Associated Press uses these rules for granting anonymity:

1. The material is information and not opinion or speculation and is vital to the news report.
2. The information is not available except under the conditions of anonymity imposed by the source.
3. The source is reliable and in a position to have accurate information.

Usually reporters grant anonymity if the source's job or safety is at risk. Before you agree to this, make sure it is clear why the source is requesting to have his or her name removed from the story. You may need to get permission from your editor before confirming anonymity with the source. You should agree with the source how exactly she or he will be identified in the story (e.g. "said a source who was at the meeting") and tell the reader why anonymity was granted (e.g. "who requested anonymity because she was afraid of retaliation from her teammates").

Notetaking

Notice how Kubble always has his reporter's notebook with him? He writes down the notes from his interviews while his colleagues at *The Hallway Monitor* record their interviews. There are pros and cons to both methods.

Handwriting or typing notes		Digitally recording	
PRO	*CON*	*PRO*	*CON*
Forces you to pay closer attention to what the source says	Awkward pauses or typing noises while the source speaks	You catch every word	You have to spend time transcribing all or parts of it
You don't have to spend time after the interview transcribing	Hard to catch every word	You have backup proof in case source counters he/she was quoted inaccurately	Easy to stop paying attention since the recorder is "listening"
Your pen probably won't run out of ink and you will find something to take notes on. You are faster at typing than you are at writing	Worst case scenario: Your pencil break, computer freezes, your pen runs out of ink or there is no paper anywhere for you to write on		Technology might fail you and you lose the interview

If possible, use both methods. Record the interview using your smartphone or an external recording device and take notes. That way you have a backup and you will avoid the "Time Technology Failed Me" story many professional journalists have.

When taking notes, reporters come up with their own shorthand so they can get the essence and the exact wording down correctly (see next page).

Immediately after the interview, while the source is still available, quickly look over your notes and see if there are any remaining questions you need the source to answer. After the interview is over, take a moment and carefully review your notes while the interview is fresh in your head. Complete partial quotes and star good quotes.

Note: While federal law requires only one person in the conversation to consent to being recorded (a.k.a., you, the reporter), states vary on this. Some states require all parties involved in the call to provide permission. Others don't. To find out what the law is in your state, consult the Recording Guide on the Reporters Committee for Freedom of the Press website. To avoid being on the wrong side of the law, make sure you have asked your source for permission to record the interview, while the recorder is on.

Shorthand Notetaking Example

B is 2 sport that builds character
Xcellent cardio workout

teens Ø enough exercise
Appeals to young ppl. of all athl. ability

Nothing like winning x rally & hearing crowd
chant YR NAME ☆

Refuse to shortchange future of students
create jobs — from construct wkrs to
concession st operators

Will pay for itself

ticket sales + ???

Donors reluctant to pay for what district should

B v. Public

Possibilities 4 corp sponsor &
naming rights ⬅

#1 SPORT AMONG Hi-schoolers in dist. ☆

popularity growing evry yr

B. cures ADHD ⬅

Why not just do the interview via email?

Email interviews tend to be boring and should be a last case scenario. Quotes that are written have less personality and sound less lively than spoken quotes. However, sometimes email interviews are the only option, especially with school administrators. In these cases, be as specific as you can be in your questions, since you won't have a chance to clarify until after the source responds.

Dixon Confesses
Election Fixed, Class Secretary Implicated
by Joe Kubble

School president Nick Dixon has admitted that he fixed the September election so he could beat rival Polly Pompa in a vote of 554 to 546.

"Mistakes were made," said Dixon, 18, in a tense interview with the Monitor last night. "I let my desire to win cloud my judgment."

Dixon, a senior, would not say if he would voluntarily step down from office, and as of press time it was unclear whether he would be stripped of his position.

"We are disappointed in this turn of events," said Principal Evens, adding that the administration will "conduct an investigation into the allegations."

Dixon said that he asked the school secretary, Sarah Snifter, to add fake names to the voting roster and count these votes in his favor. Snifter, 17, was his girlfriend at the time, both Dixon and Snifter have confirmed.

The Monitor discovered the fake names after a tip from an anonymous source. The voting lists showed the addition of 12 false Central High Students, including Angeliqua Zolie, Tomas Jefferson and Kanye East.

In an emotional interview on Wednesday, Snifter regretted her behavior.

"I was blinded by love," she said. "I feel like such an idiot."

Dixon was apologetic but wouldn't comment on the likelihood of being stripped of his title.

"I'm sorry if I betrayed those who believed in me, but I am still the most capable student to lead East Haywood High," he said.

Pompa, a 17-year-old senior and the cheerleading captain, called Dixon's fraudulent victory over her in the election a "disgrace."

"He should step down with his tail between his legs," said Pompa. "He doesn't deserve to lead a conga line, much less this school. We deserve better."

But not all students agree with Pompa.

"Dixon still gets my vote," said junior Alexis Richard, 17. "He was honest about his failings. I'm sure one misstep won't define his presidency."

Dixon ran for school president three years ago as a freshman under the slogan, "Put Someone FRESH in Office." He lost that election to Kendra Mikowlski in the most lopsided race in the school's history, 981 to 7. Since then, he has set two school records -- in overtime soccer goals and money raised in last year's dance-a-thon.

The principal has called an emergency meeting of the student council to discuss the matter in the morning. The disciplinary committee will meet later this week to consider the allegations against both Dixon and Snifter.

The Journalistic Takeaway: Verifying Tips

Seek out tips, but always check them out before using them in your story.

Deep Throat told Kubble that Nick Dixon fixed the election, but as Trixie points out, that's not enough to go on. Deep Throat could have been spreading a rumor or even making the story up to intentionally hurt Nick. Journalists never trust anyone when they're reporting a story, the saying goes: "If your mom says she loves you—check it out!" Journalists are always looking for proof. Kubble had to confirm that what Deep Throat told him was true. He needed to backup the information with facts, data, and other interviews.

Find the evidence to back up your information. Follow a "reporting trail."

In some ways, reporters are like detectives. In a courtroom, a person can't be convicted of a crime without hard evidence against them. Likewise, in journalism we can't tell stories without hard evidence. Kubble had a hunch that what Deep Throat told him about Nick Dixon was correct, but he needed to prove it before he could write his story. Nick knew this too—without any evidence against him, he knew he didn't need to confess.

To find that evidence, Kubble followed a reporting trail. When Trixie asked him, "What kind of data could show evidence of Nick cheating?," he realized he needed to get the voter lists. It took a lot of work, and help from his fellow journalists, but eventually Kubble found some fishy names on that list—students who didn't exist.

The next step on Kubble's reporting trail was to figure out who wrote the voter lists and who had access to them. He went to the person with the most information about that, Ms. Strickler, the teacher who oversaw the election. She led him to the next source, Sarah Snifter, who provided the hard evidence he needed to write the story and use to confront Nick.

Always go to the source.

For a freshman like Kubble, it's scary to confront a popular senior like Nick Dixon or even to speak to him. For a student of any age, it's intimidating to approach teachers, administrators, other students, and people on the street to ask for quotes. But it is very important in journalism to include the perspective of the key figures in the news story and to notify them in advance of publication. As Trixie says, "Nobody should ever be surprised to see their name in print."

You should make a sincere effort to speak to everyone the story mentions, so that they have an opportunity to tell you their point of view, respond to any accusations, and point out any errors in your coverage. If a source refuses to comment or does not respond to repeated requests for a quote, mention that in your story and describe how you attempted to establish contact.

The Story Behind the Story:
Watergate

"Deep Throat," the informant who told Kubble about Nick Dixon fixing his own election, has the same name as an important figure in American history. In 1972, a tipster whose alias was Deep Throat gave information to reporter Bob Woodward of *The Washington Post*, who worked with another reporter, Carl Bernstein, to break one of the biggest political and journalistic stories of last century: the Watergate scandal.

Deep Throat, whose identity was kept secret for more than 30 years, was revealed in 2005 to be a former FBI associate director named Mark Felt. He shared information with the reporters about the arrests of five men on the sixth floor of the Watergate Hotel in Washington, D.C. The men had broken into the offices of the Democratic National Committee.

There were some fishy things about these five robbers: they were carrying a large amount of cash in $100 bills, they had very sophisticated surveillance equipment, and one of the men, a former CIA employee, had a job working security for the committee to re-elect the Republican President, Richard Nixon. It soon became clear that the men were trying to steal information from the Democrats about their election efforts. The scandal, and suspicions of Nixon's involvement in the burglary, eventually led to Nixon resigning the presidency in 1974.

Woodward and Bernstein were not newbies to journalism, as Kubble is, but they were very young, both in their twenties. They got the tip from Deep Throat only after investigating the Watergate Hotel break-in, and discovering the suspicious details. Deep Throat, with his access to FBI reports on the burglary investigation, helped the young reporters by confirming and denying what other sources told them.

For Further Reference

"Watergate at 40" is *The Washington Post*'s great interactive feature telling the story of Watergate, step by step.

In 1976, only two years after Nixon resigned, the movie *All the President's Men*, starring Dustin Hoffman and Robert Redford, presented a glamorous image of journalists to Americans. It's still a classic depiction of journalism on film.

On YouTube, watch Carl Bernstein and former *Washington Post* executive editor Leonard Downie, Jr. talk about breaking the Watergate story at a screening of *All the President's Men* hosted by The Newseum.

Classroom Activities

To Consider

1. Should Kubble have named Sarah Snifter in his article, even though it might get her into trouble and make her mad at him?

This is a difficult question and there's no one right answer. On one hand, Sarah did do something wrong by fixing the voter lists, even if she did it because Nick convinced her to. Also, she told Kubble her story without him promising to keep it "off the record," so he had made no promise to keep her name secret.

But on the other hand, it's always hard to "burn a source." Kubble didn't want to hurt anyone, especially someone who, like Sarah, was an important source who helped him get his story.

As discussed previously, Bob Woodward and Carl Bernstein kept the identity of their "Deep Throat" source secret for three decades. Other journalists have gone to jail rather than reveal the names of their sources to courts.

2. Do you think Kubble did the right thing? Should Trixie have stepped in to make a case for keeping Sarah's identity secret? Write a 200-word essay making your argument.

Exercises

1. For each headline below, write a list of all the possible sources for the story.

Community Wants Post Office to Stay

Some Who Wear Hijab Feel Unsafe in the City

State Braces for Early Mosquito Invasion

2. Practice taking notes while watching the news.

Aim for at least five full direct quotes from sources quoted on the newscast and take notes summarizing each story the anchors and in-the-field reporters cover.

3. Learn interviewing from a pro.

For more than 30 years Terry Gross has interviewed newsmakers on her National Public Radio show, *Fresh Air*. Listen to an episode of the show and make a list of things you notice about her interviewing skills. What are some tactics she uses or things you notice? Aim for five to seven techniques to add to your interviewing repertoire.

What Is News?

News Values are the qualities that determine which events make good news stories. The greater the news value of a story, the more likely it will be to run on the front page of the newspaper or beginning of a news broadcast. Likewise, the facts within a story that have the greatest news value should be at the top of the story, in the lede or nut graph.

Here are the elements that will allow you to judge an idea's news value:

IMPACT or the affect of the news on people: How many people does this story affect? How deeply does it impact their lives? The more people affected on a deep level, the better the story.

CONFLICT or struggle: People are drawn to read about sports and politics because of the inherent conflict of stories with winners and losers. All good storytelling includes friction between characters or ideas. The drama of one person wanting one thing and another person wanting something else makes for a good read.

HUMAN INTEREST or a story with heart: People like to read stories that have a real heart beat to them. You don't want your stories to be sappy or too sentimental but there is nothing wrong with making readers care.

NOVELTY or newness: How new or unique is your story? A 113-year-old woman is news because she is one-of-a-kind. Likewise, an innovative approach to studying might make it to the front page because no one has done it before.

PROMINENCE or famousness: The more well-known the people in the news story are, the more your readers will want to read it. The pope, the president, your principal—these are all big names who will capture your reader's attention. Be judicious—sometimes celebrity news lacks any real relevance or impact.

PROXIMITY or closeness: You want your readers to feel connected to a story by showing them how it relates to them. The closer a story is to home, the more they are going to care. When it comes to international stories or big issue stories, like the economy or health care, your job is to localize the issue as a way to create a connection between the reader and the topic. (See "Localizing News" in this chapter.)

TIMELINESS or recentness: For news to be useful, it should have just happened, or be ongoing. Reporting the news as it happens allows readers to react to what's going on and even get involved.

Localizing News

You want to produce news for your readers that they relate to. It's easy to do this with stories about school clubs, new administrative rules or, teachers, but there is a whole world outside the school that you need to cover, too.

SCRATCH THAT.

The whole world is already **in your school**. The key is finding that connection. For example, let's say you want to do a story about girls' education access in Kenya. You are passionate about the issue and you think everyone should know that many families in Kenya will pay to send their sons to school and not their daughters. Your job as a reporter is to connect what's happening in Kenya to something or somebody at your school—a technique known as localizing a story.

Here are some ideas to localize your coverage about the education of girls in Kenya:

- Are there any students at your school who emigrated from Kenya or who have family who did?
- Find someone at the school who has done a community service trip to Kenya.
- Are there any on-site fundraising programs for international issues?
- Compare the life opportunities for a 15-year-old in your town to a 15-year-old in Kenya.
- Is there a teacher or administrator on staff with Kenyan roots who can talk about the issue?
- Are there any special classroom speakers with an expertise in gender equality in education?

The goal is to find someone in the school who is impacted by the broader issue, who has a personal connection to it, or someone has expertise on the topic. You are helping readers see how this issue impacts their specific community.

Localizing a story is a great way to come up with new story ideas. Go to a news site and see what it is covering. Is there a way to make a connection between that issue and your school? If so, you've got yourself a solid story idea!

Question Writing

Always write down your questions before an interview. This will allow you to focus on listening instead of trying to think of what to ask next. Make sure you ask questions that are within the parameters of what the source would know.

Too General: Why do teens Photoshop their Instagram photos?
More Specific: Why do you Photoshop your Instagram photos?

A teen won't necessarily know why other teens do it, but they can answer why they do it.

Great ways to start questions:

Who? What? Where? When? How? Why?
- Can you tell me about a time when..?
- When was the first/last, best/worst...?
- Describe for me a time when....?

Write down more questions than you'll need. You'll come up with a variety of interesting options when you push yourself to write 15 or 20 questions for every source. Think about the types of questions you are asking. Shake it up a little by asking the unexpected.

Man from Mars

Sometimes you know the answer, but you need the perspective of a source.

Pretend that you are from outer space and are curious about the ways of this planet.

"Why is health insurance important?"
"How big of a deal is prom at this school?"
"How do you feel when you wake up at 5:15 a.m. for school?"

Hypothetical

"What if" questions allow sources to imagine a situation outside of what is happening right now.

Sometimes the value of these questions is just to break a source's habit of answering questions without really thinking about what they are saying.

"If you could go to any college in the world, where would you go?"
"What if you had an unlimited budget for the school—what would you spend it on?"
"How would you spend your time if you had no homework?"

Statistical

Including statistics in your questions helps show your source that you have done your research, and it also makes them respond to specific facts.

Here are two examples of how to incorporate statistics into an interview:

"In my research I found that 12 states make it illegal for teens to use tanning salons. Based on your experience is this statistic up to date?"

"It is illegal for anyone under 18 to use a tanning salon in 12 states, including ours. How do you feel about that?"

Personal Experience

You can either incorporate your own personal experience into a question, or ask your source about a personal matter. Keep in mind that not every source will want to go there, so make sure to start with informational questions and then lead into more personal ones, if it is appropriate for the story and your source seems receptive.

"I let myself go online for 15 minutes as a reward for studying 45 minutes. What's your technique for staying focused when doing homework?"

"Can you tell me about how your personal experiences led you into this field of study?"

Devil's Advocate

The key with these questions is not to get confrontational. Your job isn't to upset your source; it is to present an opposite stance so as to elicit a response.

"Your opponent says your proposal to introduce metal detectors in the school is archaic. What is your comment on that?"

"Some students think the new gym policy is unfair. How do you respond that?"

Keep in Mind

It makes for a better interview if you can set-up your question with some sort of statement. It leads more naturally into the question and gives your source a little bit of context, which will also help the interview flow more naturally.

Don't be afraid to go off script in your interview. You may come up with additional questions depending on what the source tells you. Here are four excellent follow up questions:
- Can you tell me more about that?
- How did you feel when that happened?
- What were you thinking when that happened?
- Who did you talk to about it?

28

Ask "Why?" Before Writing "I"

When Tatyana says to Trixie that "There's no 'I' in team," she is focused on the fact that news stories traditionally don't have first or second-person reporting. But that doesn't mean there is no room for first-person stories in the news. Besides showing up in features, arts, and opinion sections, first-person perspective can be appropriate in news coverage.

In the left column below are a list of questions you should ask yourself before talking to your editor about using "I" in an article, the column on the right shows how Tatyana answered each question for her piece.

Why do I want to use first-person?	MAYBE MY STORY WILL BE RELATABLE TO OTHER TEENS WHO FEEL THEY ARE THE ONLY ONES DEALING WITH THE REALITIES OF A BAD ECONOMY.
What will my perspective add?	A PERSONALIZED TAKE ON A BIG PICTURE TOPIC.
What would be lost if first-person wasn't used?	IT MIGHT BE HARD TO GET THE NUANCED PERSONAL ELEMENTS ACROSS SINCE THIS IS A HARD TOPIC FOR TEENS TO TALK ABOUT.
Is my perspective unique enough to merit first-person reporting?	IT MAY NOT BE UNIQUE, BUT IT IS CERTAINLY REPRESENTATIVE AND RELATABLE.
Is there another way to get this story to the reader?	MAYBE DO AN AS-TOLD-TO PIECE? BUT GETTING TEENS TO OPEN ON ON THE PRIVATE ELEMENT OF THEIR FAMILY WILL BE CHALLENGING.

Keep in mind that first-person articles may still require reporting—statistics, research, and even supplementary quotes from experts will all work together to make a personal narrative hit home for the reader. First-person pieces can add depth and nuance to an issue in a way a news story can't, but proceed with caution. By telling your story, you're taking the place of someone else. Be alert to whose voice you are replacing.

Letting staffers share their personal histories with readers is a great way of utilizing the experiences of your newsroom. However, you may also be limiting the people who get to be heard—those who can write. One way to open the personal narrative to a wider group is by doing an "As Told To" story. These articles read as if they were written by a staff reporter, but in fact the reporter interviewed the source and collected their answers into a narrative format—a Q&A without the Q.

The Recession Is a Teen Issue, Too
By Carrie Santer
as told to Tatyana Maslani

My dad used to install solar panels. He worked 10–12 hour days climbing up and down ladders. We were never rich but we got by ok between that and my mom's job as a receptionist at a dentist office. But then the recession hit and everything fell apart.

It's hard seeing your dad out of work. He felt like he was failing us as a family and it was hard to know if everything was going to be all right. Money was tight and we all knew it. I felt bad when I had to ask my mom for money to cover school fees. I backed away from fun stuff—like going to the movies—because I didn't want to hear my mom say, "No." Or worse, feeling guilty after she gave me the cash—like it was my fault we were eating store brand Raisin Bran instead of the real stuff.

At school, I didn't tell anyone about my dad's job. It's not like that stuff comes up. Even in classes when the recession came up it was in vague terms focusing on "the country's economic health" or something like that. I pretended like we were weren't suffering at home and that it wasn't hard on me all the time.

I learned last week that my friend's mom has been out of work for a few months now. She didn't want to tell us because she was embarrassed. The thing is, my friend has it pretty bad because her dad's not around, so she has an out-of-work single mom. Which is really tough. I don't want her or other people at the school to feel bad anymore, so I thought sharing my story here would help everyone see that the recession isn't only something for newspapers and adult conversation. The recession hits us, too.

Consider the questions the reporter had to ask to get this type of detail. Follow-up questions are key in as-told-to pieces. Careful editing is a must here. You can rearrange the answers and add structure with subheads, but you never want to change the intent or the meaning of what the source told you. Your goal is to create a piece that has a narrative arc—a beginning, middle, and end—and is true to the speaker's experience.

THE HALLWAY MONITOR

ALUMNI SUPPORT LIFTS WEIGHT ROOM INTO 21ST CENTURY

by Manuel Gomez

The only thing missing from East Haywood's new weight room is the smell of sweat.

The $175,000 renovation included impact absorbing flooring, eight new exercise machine, a classroom's worth of yoga mats, and two sets of dumbbells. Alumni support, led by former professional soccer player Mia Messi, paid for the upgrade.

Coach Walker said the new facilities will give students athletes a competitive edge.

"Don't be surprised if we need a new trophy case in a couple of years," Walker said at the ribbon cutting ceremony for the weight room last week surrounded by student athletes.

The renovations extended to the locker rooms where students now have working showers.

"I feel like a prince," said quarterback Jerome Blacksmith in the dressing room after his inaugural shower.

Alumni support paid for the weight room renovation, which was carried out by AAA Construction, above.

THE RECESSION IS A TEEN ISSUE, TOO

by Tatyana Kucerova

Teachers always talk about the "real world," like teens live in bubble. Yes, there are some things we don't have to do until we're older, like pay a mortgage or navigate office politics, but that doesn't mean we aren't impacted by adult realities.

For example, the recession. In economics we learned how the housing crisis caused a recession that slowed the economy down. What we didn't learn is that how to navigate high school when your family is struggling because your dad is out of work because nobody has the money to start or finish construction jobs.

My real world isn't a protected bubble where I can let adults worry about things like college tuition or even paying for a new backpack. With my dad out of work, my family

The Journalistic Takeaway: Earn Trust with Transparency

Be open about your connection to a story.

Some school newspapers have rules about reporters covering a team or club they're part of, others don't. Either way you should be clear with your editor and your readers if you are involved in story, which might affect your ability to report objectively. Even if you think you can keep yourself out of a story, disclose the connection and you will build a better relationship with those around you.

Consider the potential ramifications.

All the choices you make for your newspaper affect the staff, the readers and the school community. Keep this in mind when deciding what stories to cover and who should cover them. Trixie introduced some risk to Tatyana's family by moving forward with the story about the weight room renovations.

What if the school board decided to pull the funding after the story ran? That would jeopardize Tatyana's father's income. How can Trixie weigh the mission of *The Hallway Monitor* against the student newsroom reality? How can an editor decide whether a particular risk is worth taking? How accurately can a newspaper gauge how likely is it that a negative consequence will occur?

Covering the track meet, for example, might not have any obvious ramifications but every school and every situation is different and the editors and reporters have to work together to make sure the decision is the right one.

Think outside of the news format.

It didn't take Trixie long to come up with an alternative version of Tatyana's story. Tatyana could still write about the issue, but now in a personal way. This ability to think outside the news format is valuable for both writers and editors.

Sometimes you'll want a fresh take on tired topic (prom, the big game, theatre production, etc.). Other times you'll want to give the reader a nuanced understanding by tagging a news story with another piece—like Trixie did with the weight room story.

One way to stay nimble is to read other student publications, local newspapers, and even college news sites. Be inspired by how news can be delivered in a variety of formats and practice bringing them to life. Not all will earn an A+ from you readers, but the key is keeping it fresh and interesting.

The Story Behind the Story:
ESPN & *League of Denial*

From the Society of Professional Journalists Code of Ethics

Act Independently

The highest and primary obligation of ethical journalism is to serve the public.

Journalists should:
- Avoid conflicts of interest, real, or perceived. Disclose unavoidable conflicts
- Refuse gifts, favors, fees, free travel, and special treatment, and avoid political and other outside activities that may compromise integrity or impartiality, or may damage credibility.
- Be wary of sources offering information for favors or money; do not pay for access to news. Identify content provided by outside sources, whether paid or not
- Deny favored treatment to advertisers, donors or any other special interests, and resist internal and external pressure to influence coverage.
- Distinguish news from advertising and shun hybrids that blur the lines between the two. Prominently label sponsored content.

In 2013, ESPN backed out from involvement in *League of Denial*, a documentary it had been producing with PBS' FrontLine about the National Football League's response to head injuries. The reasons ESPN gave were vague. Was it because it was pressured by NFL executives, as news sites reported? Or was it, as they said, because they didn't have editorial control over the content?

There was an inherent conflict ESPN producing *League of Denial*. Its reporters cover the leagues that it also pays billions of dollars to for the rights to broadcast games. The rumors surrounding ESPN concerning about the documentary put the network's integrity and independence in question.

Being free from external influence is essential to journalism. Without independence, a publication can become a mouthpiece for anybody who has enough money or leverage to purchase the platform. With independence, journalism retains its role as a champion of truth.

Classroom Activities

Beyond YES or NO Workshop

One of the challenges when writing an article is producing substantive quotes from a source. It's hard to create content around a "yes" or a "no" answer. Turn the following closed-ended questions—those that can be answered with one word—into open-ended questions, that will lead to more compelling answers.

1. Do you think the mayor is doing enough to support students with disabilities?
2. Does TV influence you?
3. Does photography make you feel better when you're down?
4. So have you guys ever heard of the new vaccine that's to prevent HPV?
5. Did the commercial suck? Was it boring?
6. Do you feel that recess should be added to schools that don't already have it?
7. Do you think the fact that there is separation between the sexes makes it more difficult for guys and girls to talk to each other?
8. Do you think that this event is helping you?
9. Do you think coming to this country affects your culture?

Write Your Own Dossier

Part of figuring out your own potential conflicts of interest as a reporter, is creating a file that lists groups, and activities, as well as individual people, that you are directly involved with.

A. Create a one-page document (maximum) about yourself that answers these questions:

1. What school club or groups do you belong to?
2. What groups or organizations outside of school are you part of?
3. Do you have a public blog or social media accounts?
4. What information is public about you? How does this information, true or false, reflect on your beliefs, interests? (You will have to research yourself online for this one.)
5. Include a list of your five closest friends.
6. Include a list of five adults you are related that have professional expertise. Indicate the expertise.

B. Based on this information provide a list of topics that your dossier would require reveal the need for increased transparency. What topics would your contacts and expertise add value to?

Hone Your News Sense

Assess these story ideas for your publication based on which news values they have. In the notes column, explain whether the news values are strong enough to make the idea into an article that will interest your readers.

	Impact	Conflict	Human Interest	Proximity	Prominence	Novelty	Timeliness	Notes
Drama department gets a donation of 1930s style dresses for its costume collection.								
Protesters outside the senator's office were tear gassed last week.								
Study reveals that only 10 percent of monuments and memorials in town honor women.								
Pope declares that house pets will go to heaven when they die.								

Localizing News

Practice localizing these news events for your audience.

News Event	Localized Idea
Country elects the world's first transgender leader	
Gas prices go up world-wide	
School bus strike in neighboring state	
National academic proficiency scores have been released	
Students in another part of the country protest school dress code	

Chapter 3:

NEW RULES
FOR A NEW
JOURNALISM
JOURNALISM IN THE 21ST CENTURY

Social Media

Social media can be a journalist's best friend. Here are some ways it can enhance your reporting.

Identifying Trends

Keep an eye on what people are talking about online. This could help you identify trends and potential story ideas. What hashtags are people using? What conversations are going viral? Not everything you see online will make a good story, but as a reporter you need to keep your finger on the pulse of what's happening.

Finding Sources

For school newspapers, finding teen sources can be as easy as walking into the lunchroom. Other times, students may not be as forthcoming and it takes some online searching to discover who is into online gaming or who volunteers at the local soup kitchen. Social media sleuthing can help you find a professional on a topic that is not directly related to your school, too. Outside sources add legitimacy and relevance to your articles, so it is worth the extra step to find and approach them.

Finding News and Reaction

When something unexpected or unplanned happens, a.k.a. breaking news, social media can be both your news source and place to get reaction. Let's say a main road to your school closes for construction. You may first find out about it through a post online. Follow the comment thread to get students' reaction to the inconvenience.

Part of the value of using social media in reporting is that is an open marketplace of quotations that can act as a litmus test of a community. But because journalism is a practice based on verification, you want to confirm people's identities and experiences when possible. Posting on social media is a form of publishing in the public domain, but that doesn't mean it's a free for all. Do your due diligence and fact check.

Building Loyalty

Becoming a source of trusted information will help you cultivate a network of readers and sources. This bond connects you to the community you serve and will help you create a brand for yourself as a reporter.

Sharing Your Work

Once your article is complete, head to social media to share it with the world. Make sure to tag sources in your post and use appropriate hashtags. Don't hesitate to share bigger stories with local media as well. Be proud of your work and amplify the stories you tell through social media.

Many professional news agencies have strict guidelines about what their reporters can post on their social media accounts.

"Conduct yourself online just as you would in any other public circumstances as an NPR journalist. Treat those you encounter online with fairness, honesty and respect, just as you would offline. Verify information before passing it along. Be honest about your intent when reporting. Avoid actions that might discredit your professional impartiality. And always remember, you represent NPR."

—National Public Radio's Ethic Handbook

ANATOMY OF A NEWS STORY

HEADLINE —
FEMALE TEENS COSPLAY FOR SELF-EXPRESSION, COMMUNITY

BYLINE — By Fareen Ali, 19
Women's eNews, March 27, 2017

LEDE — SANTA BARBARA, Calif.– In a photograph taken earlier this year, 14-year-old Eliza Garcia is looking over her left shoulder, wearing a blue-green ball gown she sewed herself, out of a corset and old ballet tutu.

LEDE QUOTE — This is more than just a photo of Garcia in a pretty dress though. This is cosplaying, "an art form beyond simply 'dressing up,'" she said from her home in Orange County, California. In the photo Garcia is dressed as Eliza Hamilton, a character from the Broadway show "Hamilton."

NUT GRAF — Cosplay, or "costume play," is when people dress up to resemble a character or persona from a book, TV show, movie, video game or other forms of entertainment. More than 60 percent of cosplayers are female, **ATTRIBUTION** — according to a 2013 study published in the journal Intensities, which polled 966 cosplayers between the ages of 13 and 74.

Many young women are attracted to cosplay as it allows for self-expression and also provides community and entertainment.

DIRECT QUOTE — "Even if I'm putting on the clothes and character of someone else, I've never felt more myself," said Garcia.

Ishmam Tanveer, 16, describes cosplaying as a way to "step into the shoes of my character and see how they would view the world," she said from her home in Oaksville, Ontario. Tanveer often cosplays as Feferi Peixus from the webcomic "Homestuck" and Princess Jasmine from Disney's "Aladdin."

INTERRUPTED QUOTE — Ferferi Peixus' "adorable demeanor and how she reacts to situations reminds me a lot of myself," says Tanveer, drawing connections between herself and the character she cosplays as. Tanveer also admires Princess Jasmine's character. "Her idea of not being 'better' than others is a favorite of mine," she said. "She's just so strong and witty!"

Sense of Community

TRANSITION — Like Tanveer, some cosplayers are drawn to characters' strong personalities because they feel like they can either relate to them or because they look up to them.

PROOF — Olivia Hale, from Surrey, U.K., often cosplays as Lara Croft from the video game "Tomb Raider." "I love her personality; how persistent she is and determined," the 15-year-old said. "I like showing multiple personas, both strong and sweet. And not being viewed as less of a woman for it."

Hale finds a sense of community from other cosplayers, too. "I just found a lot of people that I get on really well with through it."

PARAPHRASED QUOTE — Cosplay can also provide an escape for young girls from societal expectations, said Andrea Letamendi, one of the psychologists who conducted the 2013 study. "Being able to access the traits of a fictional character-features such as boldness, courage, anger, aggression and sensuality-in an acceptable context such as cosplay can allow young girls to feel validated and even help them develop emotional literacy."

Letamendi is also a cosplayer and the presenter of the TEDx presentation "Capes, Cowls and Courage: The Psychological Power of Superheroes."

Cosplaying can also help with combating low self-esteem. "It was really comforting to put on a costume and think, hey, I look pretty as this character, and then see the same beauty when I took the costume off and return to being me," said 18-year-old Emilia Sunderland. Now the Seattle Pacific University first-year cosplays for escapism. She calls it an enjoyable "break from life's problems."

Facing Backlash

BUT GRAPH — However, while character appreciation and female empowerment are linked to cosplay, so is infantilization and harassment, added Sunderland.

"Lots of people assume I'm into certain fetishes…which isn't the case. I find that really disgusting and dehumanizing. I'm 18 and I deserve the respect you would give a young adult," she said. "My friends and I have all had to deal with pedophiles and/or weird stalkers at some point. As a teenage girl, you always have to be careful."

"Women are more likely to experience catcalling, groping and inappropriate comments," said Jillian Trinh, 18, from San Jose, California. "People who do that assume that those women are asking for and expecting that kind of attention."

While some cosplayers face backlash based on gender, others face backlash based on ethnicity. Britany Marriott, a Jamaican and African American professional cosplayer said, "'There are times where people have said I was 'inaccurate' because I cosplayed traditional Japanese anime characters…Of course I do not look Japanese but that doesn't stop me from cosplaying a character who I love without disrespecting a race."

KICKER — Garcia herself was hesitant about cosplaying as characters that weren't Filipino. "At first I was afraid of dressing up as someone with a different ethnic background, but I soon realized that it didn't matter. It also showed the little representation of some minorities in the media."

VOICE OF AUTHORITY

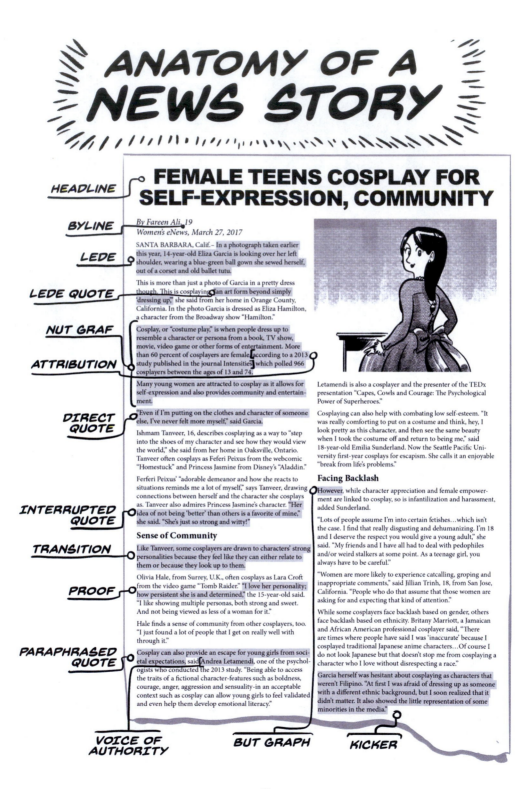

Anatomy of a News Story

The Parts of a News Story

Headline—The "title" of a news story.

Byline—Tells the reader who wrote the story, who it is "by."

Lede—The first paragraph or two in the story. This article uses an anecdotal lede. Summary news ledes get to the who, what, when and where right away, but may not be the most interesting for the reader. The job of the lede is to grab the reader's attention with the truth. (See "Ledes" in this chapter.)

Nut graf—This is the sentence in the story that tells the reader what the story is about. It is the story in a nutshell. It tells the reader the who, what, when, where. The rest of the story delves into the why and the how. Another way of looking at it, according to Betty Ming Liu, a professor at New York University, is that the nut graf gives readers a sense of **What Was, What's New, What's Now.** For some news stories, the lede and the nut graph are the same thing. For other feature stories, or for stories that don't use a news lede, then the nut graf is further down in the story the second or third paragraph.

Even before you begin writing your piece, try summarizing the results of reporting. This helps you focus the piece and can feed into your nut graf. It's deeper than asking yourself what the story is about. What did you, as the reporter, find out?

Lede quote—The first quote in the story. Often the most powerful quote.

Types of quotes—direct, paraphrase, partial, interrupted.

Proof—Documentation provided in the form of quotations, research citations, and statistics.

Attribution—Tells the reader where information comes from and provides transparency. In most cases use "said" or "says." Readers are so used to "said" that it becomes almost like punctuation. Using other words draws attention away from the story.

Context/background—Gives a wider frame through which to understand the story.

Voice of Authority—An outside, expert voice that can provide context and speak to the implications of the issue.

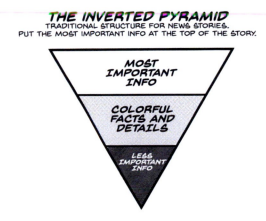

THE INVERTED PYRAMID
TRADITIONAL STRUCTURE FOR NEWS STORIES.
PUT THE MOST IMPORTANT INFO AT THE TOP OF THE STORY.

MOST IMPORTANT INFO

COLORFUL FACTS AND DETAILS

LESS IMPORTANT INFO

Transitions—Transitions carry the reader from one thought to the next. Pronouns and transitional words (however, but, after, before, etc.) do a good job of this. Using transitions to set up the upcoming quote, often by paraphrasing or categorizing a conept, is a good way to keep the reader on track.

But graph—the graph that shows the other side or another point of view. e.g. "However, proponents claim the plan is valid."

Kicker—end of the story, very often a quote. Goal is to kick the reader out of the story, versus a conclusion that keeps the reader wrapped up in the piece. If not a quote, try using something that looks forward to a next step or a next meeting.

"FEDDER SAID SOMETHING TO THE GUARD... ...AND NEXT THING I KNEW HE WAS THROWN ON THE GROUND... ... AND THE GUARD HAS HIS FOOT HOLDING HIM DOWN.

Ledes

The lede may not be the first part of the story the reader sees (that's the headline), but it's the first time the writer has the chance to hold the reader's attention.

Even though the lede is the first few paragraphs of an article, it doesn't need to be the first thing you write. But it should be the part of the story you spend the most time on. Before you write a lede, decide what type of lede you will write. This is an important step—otherwise you end up with an introduction. Introductions side step their way into a topic and can rely on generalizations. Ledes jump right in. Feet first.

One Story: Six Different Ledes

Teen girls get less exercise than adolescent boys, according to a new study. **News/summary**	Mason Tyler, a high school senior, doesn't have time to exercise anymore. "The last time I walked more than a mile was when my car broke down," she said. "I used to exercise way more when I was younger. I got busier." **Anecdotal**
Mason Tyler laces up her sneakers and pulls her hair back with bandana. As she walks out the front door of her apartment building, she considers whether she has time to walk the two miles to her SAT prep. She checks her phone for the time. She's running late. The bus wins. **Descriptive**	Mason Tyler exercises her right not to be physically active. "The last time I walked more than a mile was when my car broke down," she said. "I used to exercise way more when I was younger. I got busier." **Wordplay**
SAT prep. Chorus rehearsal. Shelter volunteering. Mason Tyler has lots of activities on her schedule, but exercise isn't one of them. "The last time I walked more than a mile was when my car broke down," she said. "I used to exercise way more when I was younger. I got busier." **List Lede**	Fewer than 9 percent of teens get the recommended daily amount of physical activity. **Startling Statement**

No matter what type of lede you choose, it should be based on your original reporting. Showcase the work you did—don't rehash old news or provide background in the lede. Save that for further down the piece.

Tip: If you are having trouble writing a lede, then write two ledes instead! It takes the pressure off of you to write something perfect and then you can pick which suits the article (and your editor) better.

Lazy Ledes

Your lede should not…

- **Be a question**

   …Surest way to turn the reader off. If you ask the reader a question and the answer is "no," then what?

- **Be a quote**

   …From the reader's perspective, this is the equivalent of walking into a room mid-conversation. It's not clear who is saying what and why anyone should care. This applies to both famous quotes and to quotes from sources.

- **Talk directly to the reader**

   …at least for a news story. Features pieces have more freedom with 2nd and 1st person.

"Burying the Lede/Lead"

You can decide if you want to call it a "lede" or a "lead." "Lede" is journalism jargon that derived from the days of old printing machines. Either way, it's the top of your article. If your editors tell you that you "buried the lede," they mean you hid the news by promoting unimportant details. To fix this, dig through your text for the news of the article and replant it in the first or second paragraph.

Take a Closer Look

Like all of journalism, lede writing is a craft that you will get better at the more you practice it. But no matter how many years you've been in the newsroom, you rarely get your best lede right off the bat. Crafting a good lead is a careful process that sometimes requires you to try a lot of things that don't work before you find something that does. You'll know when you have a good start when your lede is accurate, concise, specific, and compelling. Reading your work out loud can help identify hiccups in your writing. If you stumble over the words, so will your reader. A clear sign to rewrite.

On the next two pages are some examples of writers' first draft ledes and the final versions. Coaching from an editor can help elevate your writing, but you can also learn to edit yourself.

First Draft	Final Draft	Why It's Better
Teen girls go to the tanning salon because they think they look good when with tanned skin but in reality they are killing themselves.	Teens are finding their way around laws in 12 states that make it illegal for anyone under 18 to use indoor tanning facilities. With or without their parents' knowledge some teens are walking into salons and exposing themselves to ultraviolet radiation that can increase their risk of the skin cancer melanoma by 20 percent in just one visit, according to the Skin Cancer Foundation.	The final version tells the news of the article with specific details and doesn't rely on generalizations or sensationalist tactics.
On May 19, 2018 the Brown High School held its annual carnival celebration.	The bull riding is what did it for senior Kerry Bianca. "This carnival was the best one yet," said Bianca, still red-face from her 12-second adventures on the mechanical bovine at Brown High School's 7th annual carnival celebration.	Yes, the original lede has the who, what, and when but it's not interesting. Dates don't read easily and there is no reason to put it first thing in the lede unless the date offers some significance of the story itself. Let people tell the story of the article and you can fill in the details once the reader is hooked.
Haiti, a small island in the Caribbean, was damaged by a earthquake in 2010 and since then many Haitians have been giving Temporary Protected Status in the U.S. That is about to change.	Thirty-two Haitian Shelby students are at risk of deportation after the White House announced last week that their immigration was at risk.	Background information is always important in a news story but it doesn't belong in the lede. Start with the news.
As Olivia Shinzawa, a Park West sophomore who ran for the Lincoln City Council this past November, reflected on her progressive campaign, she recognized that underneath her election day loss prevails an encouraging victory: young women realizing their capability to run for political office.	After spending most of the past six months campaigning for local office, 18-year-old Olivia Shinzawa decided to celebrate her election day loss instead of mourn it.	See how the new lede places the action in the present even it were caused by something in the past? It's also shorter and sharper.

First Draft	Final Draft	Why It's Better
Eager students, parents and alumni filled the auditorium patiently waiting for the winter concert to begin. The first piece, "One Hundredth Choral," by Bourgeois blew the audience away.	Just when the audience thought the winter concert couldn't get any better, reality television star and Eagles Academy alumni Dylan McPhee stormed the stage with his signature banjo and led the auditorium in a rousing rendition of the school's anthem.	Although you experienced the event chronologically, it doesn't mean the reader has to. Start with something that happened that was interesting. Don't start at the beginning. (Also how does the reporter know they were eager if they were patiently waiting?)
In December 2015, 21 young people, ages eight to 19, filed a constitutional climate lawsuit with the help of Our Children's Trust.	It is a case of teens vs. the government. A group of 21 young plaintiffs who filed a climate change lawsuit against the federal government is about to have their day in court. The lead plaintiff, Kelsey Cascadia Rose Juliana, was 19 when the case was filed more than two years ago with the help of Our Children's Trust, an Oregon-based organization.	Too many numbers. Try reading the original version out loud. There are 21 syllables of numbers in the first 10 words. It's easy to get tripped up over the numbers. Even visually, the concentration of numbers pushes the reader away.

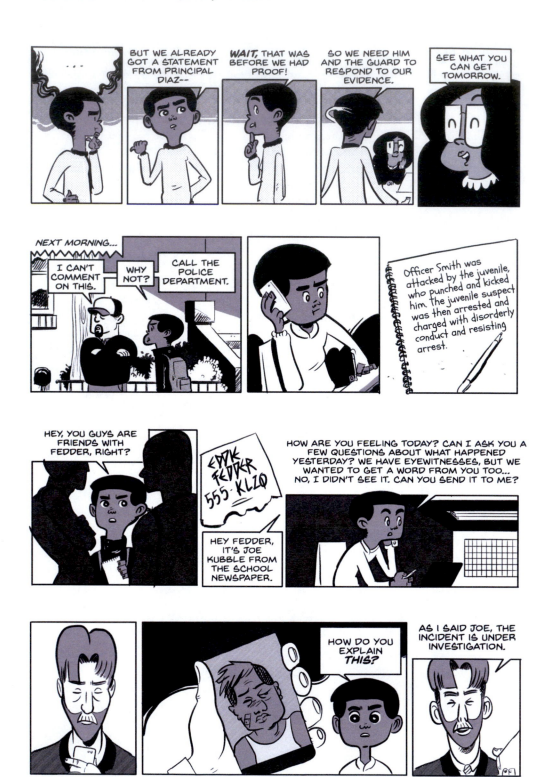

Quotations

"After conducting interviews and compiling the replies, how do you decide what quotations warrant incorporating into your news story? Your best options will shed light on the topic succinctly, but also add personality. Quotations humanize stories and make articles relatable, so you want strong selections that add life and dimension to your piece.

As the writer, you will decide what to leave out, what to paraphrase, and what to quote. Facts and statistics don't normally require direct quoting (but they do require attribution). Good quotes share uncommon knowledge, or present common knowledge in a compelling way. They reveal something about the person who said it. This is why spoken quotes are better than written ones—they have more character and are less formal.

All your quotes should be dynamic—they should emphasize something you've written previously in the article, but not repeat it. Don't save your best quote for the end of your article. Your reader may never get that far. Use it high up in your article to capture and hold your reader's attention. And while readers love quotations, you want to make sure you don't give them a monologue. Aim for using no more than 2–3 short sentences at a time. If there is good material in a lengthier quote, paraphrase most of it and let the direct quote pack the punch.**"**

Stick with Said

A thesaurus can be your friend as a writer, but when it comes to attributing quotes, only use "said" or "says." Steer clear of "explained," "exclaimed," "declared," "stated," "added," etc. "Said" and says" are neutral and unobtrusive. It may feel redundant to write, but for the reader these words are as natural as punctuation. They objectively inform the reader who said the quotation, without implying how it was said.

Take a look at the quotes in the "Anatomy of a News Story" earlier in this chapter.
- What do you notice about them?
- How long are they?
- How are they ordered? What do they add to the story the writer is telling?

TheHallwayMonitor.org

Breaking News: Guard Attacks Student

By Joe Kubble

Additional reporting by Tatyana Kucerova, Manuel Gomes, Roland Haverford Jr. and Alex Jurcisek

On Tuesday morning junior Eddie Fedder tried to bum a cigarette from school security guard Simon Patrickson. Minutes later he was face down on the sidewalk with a bloody lip and black eye. According to video from eyewitnesses, Patrickson's foot held the senior down, despite pleas from the crowd for him to let up.

"All I wanted was a smoke and the guy flipped out," said Fedder, a few hours after being released from police custody.

The police department charged Fedder with disorderly conduct and resisting arrest. But the videos, which start when Fedder first approaches the guard and continue until he is loaded into a police cruiser, show no such aggression from Fedder.

Patrickson denied any wrongdoing: "I'm on the right side of the law," he said during a phone interview from his home the afternoon of the incident. "Whatever video you have doesn't show the whole story."

Principal Diaz said "the incident is under investigation" so he couldn't say if there had been any previous instance of assault by Patrickson or Fedder.

The Hallway Monitor will continue to follow the investigation.

Surveys and Polls

Aim for Accuracy

If you survey 18 students and all 18 say they want a longer school day, does that mean everyone in your school wants a longer day? That depends on the size of your school.

The people you include in a poll is known as your sample, and the number of people in the sample is known as your sample size. The more people you poll, the more representative your selection of people will be of the school, and the more accurate your results will be. The standard sample size for high school newspapers should be 10–20 percent of the student population. So in a school of 400 students, you'll need to poll at least 40 students to get a representative sample.

Margin of Error

The only way to be certain that your survey results are completely representative of the whole school is to survey every student. Any time you go for a representative sample, there is a risk that the sample may not reflect the whole. This risk is known as a margin of error (MOE).

Professional newsrooms aim for a MOE of less than 5 percent. This means that they are 95 percent certain that their sample size represents the total population. In a school of 400 students, you'd have to interview 195 students to get a MOE of 5 percent. That may seem prohibitive in your student newsroom. You and your editor can decide what your publication is comfortable with. The key is making sure you are transparent with your reader about the sample size and MOE. You can find MOE Calculators online to help figure out the sample size.

Total population	Sample size	Margin of error
400	40	15%
400	80	10%
400	100	9%

Here are some things to keep in mind:

- Your sample should also represent the variations within the whole—ratio of male to female students, or freshmen to sophomores. You want the demographics of the survey participants to match the demographics of the school. If you are only polling honors students, then your results aren't representative of the school as a whole.

- Aim for a random selection of people to poll in order to end up with results that are truly representative of the school Make sure you are not only collecting data from one segment of the school. Try standing in one spot and asking every third person to complete the survey or go the cafeteria when you know it'll be the most mixed among classes.
- Be sure your questions use neutral wording. You don't want your expectations to sway people's answers and the outcome of the survey.
- Make it clear to the students whether the survey is anonymous or not.
- Collect some demographic data that might make results interesting. Age, race, neighborhood are good ones to start with.
- Be transparent with the reader when it comes to the number of people surveyed and the questions asked.
- Just like with interview questions, good survey questions will be specific. Instead of asking, "Do you drink coffee?" Ask, "How many cups of coffee have you had in the past week?"
- Pre-test your survey on a handful of people before you send it out. This will help you determine which questions were hard to understand or if you need to change the order of the questions. It will also give you ideas for questions to add, such as follow-up questions to clarify other answers. Also test how long the survey takes—the longer it is, the less likely people are to want to take it.

Once you've collected the information:

1. SORT THE DATA BASED ON THE DEMOGRAPHIC DATA YOU COLLECTED.

GENDER

HONORS

GRADES

2. DETERMINE WHETHER THE SAMPLE IS REPRESENTATIVE OF YOUR SCHOOL.

COFFEE IN TERMS

EAST HAYWARD HIGH SCHOOL

3. DRAW CONCLUSIONS THAT ARE PROVEN BY THE DATA YOU COLLECTED. JUST BECAUSE 20 PERCENT OF YOUR STUDENT BODY IS DRINKING COFFEE EVERY DAY, IT DOESN'T MEAN THEY AREN'T GETTING ENOUGH SLEEP. IT JUST MEANS THEY DRINK OFFEE DAILY. YOU'D HAVE TO ASK THEM WHY THEY DRINK COFFEE, HOW MUCH SLEEP THEY'RE GETTING, AND HOW TIRED THEY ARE, IF YOU WANT TO KNOW.

What about web polls?

Simple, one-question web polls are fun, easy, and interactive but, because anyone can answer, as often as they'd like, there is no true random selection. That doesn't mean they aren't useful though, especially for sensitive questions people might not want to answer directly to a fellow student. One idea for an online school poll would involve randomly selecting people to come to a computer room and anonymously fill out a poll asking about sex, drinking, racism, or substance abuse.

The Journalistic Takeaway: Audience Participation in News Gathering

Your audience is more than just readers.

They can be news collectors and news finders for you. Crowdsourcing the way *The Hallway Monitor* did is an invaluable way for reporters to collect news when they can't be on the scene. It also brings readers behind the scenes and lets them be part of the news gathering process. This strengthens the bonds your audience will have with the publication.

Audience participation doesn't have to be limited to breaking news. Instead of doing a reported piece on the breakfast habits of students at your school, have people send you photos of their morning meal. Make news fun for your community. You can always do a deeper investigative piece later on the overall a.m. nutrition of the student body.

Verify reader's work.

Reader provided video and photos aren't immediately publishable. You want to compare the materials collected to confirm that the content wasn't altered. Through follow-up interviews you can also verify the authenticity of the footage and get additional quotes.

Stay clearheaded.

Your first obligation is to the facts. The value journalists provide in an upsetting or emotional setting is dispassion. You're trying to find out what happened, later you can find out why and how people feel about it. But first you need to determine the facts, in an impartial manner without leaping to premature conclusions.

Give all a chance to respond.

In the early minutes of breaking news, the best way you can serve your readers is to create a clear path of communication. This means speaking with all the sources directly involved. This might lead to a "he said/she said" scenario, but at least you'll be stepping into the reporting on the right foot. You'll have time later to do more analysis and investigative work. But for the sake of a starting with good information, make sure all parties get an opportunity to respond—even if they don't take it.

The Story Behind the Story: Crowd Sourcing in Reporting

In Paul Lewis' fantastic TED Talk "How mobile phones helped solve two murders," *The Guardian* reporter talks about solving a murder using readers as "co-producers." By sending a general request via Twitter for witnesses of a death during a G20 protest in London, he was able to track down video footage that proved the police were responsible for a bystander's death.

This ability of citizens to be journalists helped shine a light on police mistreatment in the Arab world in 2011. It was impossible for the news media alone to cover the story as thoroughly as it deserved and as quickly as the events unfolded. "Al Jazeera was overwhelmed," the network's former general manager Wadah Khanfar said. "We had maybe three to four correspondents on the ground. There was no way we could cover a movement that size." When the thousands of protesters began uploading posts on social networking site, they became the de facto press of the **Arab Spring**, building community, documenting events, and amplifying voices. While crowdsourcing the revolution didn't lead to long-standing change in any of the countries, social media sparked a flame that spread throughout the region.

There is also an important lesson to be learned about crowdsourcing from the **Boston Marathon bombing** in 2013. After the FBI jumped on the crowdsourcing bandwagon and asked eyewitnesses to send in their images from the event, another "investigation" was started by amateur sleuths. The citizen detectives thought they had their suspect identified. *The New York Post* even put the "suspects" on the front page later that week.

But it was a false ID, prompted by fear-based accusations of online commentators, who were suspicious of the heavy looking backpack of a high school sophomore. The FBI knew nothing of the "suspects," but they did still get valuable intelligence through their request. By not verifying the information, *The New York Post* put hurt the reputation of innocent people and put the real investigation at risk.

"The traditional media could play an enormously valuable role here by separating fact from fiction and providing verified, trustworthy information," a *Forbes* article stated. "Instead, most outlets just repeated false claims made online—providing a megaphone to statements that never should have seen the light of day in the first place."

The responsibility of the media isn't just to report what's being said, it's to provide verification of rumors and suspicions. And there is a role for citizen journalists in that step. As Lewis says, "that process of witnessing, recording and sharing is called journalism and we can all do it."

Classroom Activities

Survey

Let's say one of Trixie's reporters wanted to survey the students at East Haywood High on their sleep habits. The reporter ran her survey questions past Trixie:

Do you get enough sleep?
Why don't you get enough sleep?

Trixie told her to try again with more detailed questions.

1. **List some questions you would suggest she ask students.**

2. **What demographic information should the reporter gather?**

3. **In a school of 989 students, how many should the reporter survey to get a fairly representative group?**

4. **Explain how you came up with the number and justify your margin of error.**

Ledes

Pick three news articles from either the most recent edition of your school newspaper or news site or from your local newspaper. Identify what type of lede the journalist used and then write an alternative lede. Aim for writing three different type of ledes all together.

Social Media

Pick a story from your student newspaper or a local news site. Write four social media posts that promote the story in 140 and 280 characters (two posts each for each character counts). Look to the headline, quotes, and nut graf for inspiration on how to get your audience reading.

Know Your Parts

Dissect the articles you used for the other exercises on this page. Identify the key parts of a news story.

Quote Capture

Highlight the direct quotes from this transcript you would use in your article.

Social Security Reform
Based on an interview by Children's PressLine

Children's PressLine: Why are you getting social security?

Kyle Smythe, 14: 'Cause my father's disabled. He fell off a tractor at the age of seven, and he's been diagnosed with a spinal disease and arthritis. He's physically disabled. He can hardly walk sometimes, and my mom is unable to work also.

CPL: How long have you been getting social security benefits?

K: Seven years.

CPL: How long are you going to be receiving it? When do you stop receiving the money?

K: When I'm 18. Unless I'm in college, and then it stops at 21 or 23.

CPL: How much money do you get?

K: There's $123 a month, for me. My dad and my mom get disability checks, too, and so does my brother, 'cause he's been diagnosed with bipolar. Altogether it's something like $1,200 a month.

CPL: What is the money used for?

K: It's used to pay for my clothes and my food. If you saw me and my brother, we eat a lot, 'cause we're growing teenagers. It's used for school supplies that we need every once in a while. We get extra, but a lot of times it's for stuff we need basically.

CPL: How many people are in your household in total?

K: Six.

CPL: How many of them depend on social security?

K: My mom and dad have just adopted my little niece and nephew, so they're not biologically my little brother and sister, but they soon will be receive social security like the rest of us do.

CPL: Do you feel that the money you receive is enough to pay for all your expenses?

K: We get by every month. There's always things that we could use, so every little bit helps.

CPL: If you got any extra money, what would it be used for?

K: It would be used to help us get by in the month, without wondering whether we're going to eat well. If we had more money it would be used to make sure that we had better transportation. Our car needs to be fixed. Also helping us buy more food, 'cause my niece and nephew have been added onto the family for a while now. My niece is six and my nephew is three.

CPL: Have you ever had to make personal sacrifices because your social security money wasn't enough?

K: Oh yes, plenty of sacrifices. I mean, I've always got what I needed for school, 'cause if we don't have what we need for school somebody's always there to help us. We have friends and stuff. Yeah, I had to make sacrifice by not having extra stuff that I would want to. But it's good sacrifices, 'cause I know it's helping my little niece and nephew. I've lost my bedroom because they have to share a room. My mom and dad share a room, and me and my brother share a room. I've had to give up a little bit of extra stuff, but I know it's good sacrifices cause it benefits my niece and nephew, who I wouldn't give them up for anything else in the world.

CPL: Have you ever considered getting a job during the summer to help support your family?

K: I had a job at the end of 8th going onto 9th. It was through a program called About Face for kids who don't make enough money—that need a little bit extra. I worked at the airport. I paid for my clothes and my shoes for school that year, which helped my mom and dad out. I've tried to get a job at McDonald's and Winn-Dixie down the street, but they wouldn't hire me cause they said they were tired of hiring 13-year-olds, 'cause they don't think they're responsible enough. When I turn 16 I'm definitely going to get a job.

CPL: The President has created a new social security reform. What it does is that it takes a lot of money that for social security and invests it in the stock market. How do you feel this affects you?

K: If we didn't have social security money we wouldn't be able to do a lot of things that we've been wanting to do. Also, we would be able to have money to eat, buy clothes, or anything that we need. But, if he spends it on stocks doesn't that that's sometimes helps other people? We're not getting enough money now so if plays games with the money, we might end up getting less than what we need and it'll hurt us in the long run.

CPL: Is there anything else you would like to add to the interview?

K: I'd have to say that I'd really like to talk to the president 'cause I'd like to tell him what's on my mind. Not in a bad way, cause I respect him with everything. I even wanted to vote for him if I could, but just the things that's been happening and going lately. I just wish I could talk to him. I've only got two years of high school left. I've had a rough life, but I mean it's good. I've been getting what I need, but without extra money and stuff. It's been hard for me to go on class trips and I want to get a car like all my friends at school, and that leaves me depressed and everything. That's basically all I can add, and I won't be able to go to college without scholarships. If he was still physically fit like he used to be, it would be different. He used to work for the city. He was a supervisor. He used to watch people do work, and just get paid for it 'cause he knew what he was doing. But, after he got hurt that left him really bad, and left our family messed up because he was hurt.

CPL: Okay. Thank you for participating in this interview.

K: Thank you.

- **Write an anecdotal lede based off of the transcript of Kyle's interview, with an aim to paraphrase his situation concisely and include at least one quote.**

Chapter 4:

THE POWER OF JOURNALISM

MAKING A DIFFERENCE AND MAKING A CHANGE

BREADED TILAPIA AND CAULIFLOWER MOUSSE

Students Reject, Resent 'Healthy' School Lunches
by Lolinda Bennett
The day after school officials confronted the kitchen head about compliance with federal lunch standards, students responded to the vegetable-heavy lunches with growling stomachs. Garbage cans overflowed with uneaten meals students called "gross," unappetizing" and "ugly."

HOW'S IT GOING, MS. P.?

TODAY: VEGGIE PATTY WITH BEANS!

OH, YOU KNOW, DEARY. I'M FOLLOWING ORDERS BUT I'M WORRIED THAT THE KIDS AREN'T LIKING *ANY* OF THE NEW MENU ITEMS.

I'M LOOKING FORWARD TO TRYING IT. I *LOVE* VEGGIE BURGERS.

LET'S GO TO *PIZZA PETE'S*. I CAN'T *EAT* THIS STUFF.

IS IT *THAT* BAD?

WORSE THAN YESTERDAY.

POOR MS. PICKLES. SHE'S TRYING *SO HARD* TO FEED US. MAYBE WE DON'T LIKE VEGETABLES.

I DON'T KNOW ABOUT THAT. I EAT *A TON* OF VEGETABLES AT HOME.

ME, TOO! MY MOM MAKES THIS AWESOME SPINACH LASAGNE. I SWEAR, I EAT HALF THE PAN.

YOU SHOULD TRY THE SQUASH SOUP MY DAD MAKES.

MY SISTER WOULD BE ALL OVER THAT. CAN YOU GET ME THE RECIPE?

SURE, IF YOU BRING ME A PIECE OF THE SPINACH LASAGNA NEXT TIME YOUR MOM MAKES IT?

HA! DEAL!

Newswriting

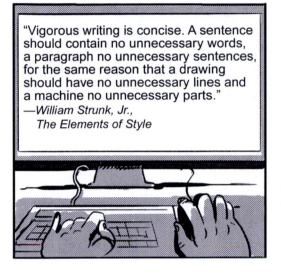

"Vigorous writing is concise. A sentence should contain no unnecessary words, a paragraph no unnecessary sentences, for the same reason that a drawing should have no unnecessary lines and a machine no unnecessary parts."
—*William Strunk, Jr.,*
The Elements of Style

Journalistic writing is distinct: Paragraphs are short and sentences are concise and direct. Your goal is to communicate the necessary information to the reader as succinctly as possible. When writing, ask yourself: Do I need every word in this sentence? Pretend like there is a word drought and your job is to use the fewest number of words to get your point across.

Examples

✗ Many young women feel an attraction to step dancing due to the fact it creates an opportunity for self-expression and also provides community and entertainment.
✓ Many young women are attracted to step dancing because of the self-expression, community, and entertainment it provides.

✗ The school board arrived at a decision to give their approval to Principal Evens to launch a fundraising campaign to raise money so the school can build a badminton court on the campus.
✓ The school board approved a fundraising campaign by Principal Evens for a $10 million Olympic-style badminton court.

✗ Sarah Johnson is a 17-year-old girl and she has a friend who is gay.
✓ Sarah Johnson, 17, has a gay friend.

✗ In Allen's case, his dream school is Boston University, which, according to him, would cost his family $66,000.
✓ Going to his dream school, Boston University, would cost Allen's family $66,000.

Active verbs, varied sentence structure, and focused paragraphs are the key to news writing. One sentence paragraphs are sometimes acceptable. So are simple words. Save your $3 words for your SAT. Don't try to sound fancy or formal. Oh, and avoid generalizations. Live long. Write Short.

Keep Moving Forward
News readers are busy people. You want to keep their attention by being efficient, not dramatic. One way to do this is to make sure every sentence tells the reader something new.

Word Choice

What do you notice about these two statements?

CATCH THE DIFFERENCE!

The Relaxers Club has received a lot of mean messages on social media from people who don't like them even though they are minding their own business.

It's not unusual for The Relaxers Club to receive criticism. Their members frequently are called "lazy" on Facebook and recently the president received an unsigned note in his mailbox: "Get off the couch, you giant waste of flesh."

IN THE FIRST STATEMENT, CAN YOU TELL WHOSE SIDE THE WRITER IS ON? HOW ABOUT IN THE SECOND? UNLESS YOU ARE WRITING A FIRST-PERSON PIECE, THE READER SHOULDN'T KNOW HOW YOU FEEL ABOUT THE TOPIC. THIS ISN'T TO SAY YOU CAN'T SHOW COMPASSION AND HUMANITY IN YOUR WRITING, BUT BE NEUTRAL AND STICK TO THE FACTS. RELY ON DESCRIPTIVE WRITING, BE SPECIFIC, AND SAVE THE EDITORIALIZING FOR THE EDITORIAL PAGE.

Even in your feature stories, keep your voice neutral.

✗ "We're going to state!," she exclaimed.

✓ "We're going to state!," she said with a grin.

or

✓ "We're going to state!," she said while pumping her fist in the air.

The second two sentences do a better job of describing her enthusiasm.
This helps the reader see the source as a three-dimensional human being.

Adjectives are another opportunity to supply readers with specific details

✗ He is a short dancer so has to work hard to keep up.

✓ His 5'4" frame makes it hard for him to cover as much ground with his leaps as his taller teammates.

The first version is too general and could mean a lot of different things to readers. The second version provides a detail that they can visualize as they read. The details act as proof—the goal is **show, don't tell**. Consider that what seems short to you, might seem tall to someone else.

THE HALLWAY MONITOR

SPINACH WINS THE GOLD!
BRUSSELS SPROUTS ARE DEFINITE LOSERS

by Lolinda Bennett

Based on the number of spinach recipes students and staff sent to The Hallway Monitor in response to an online request, the leafy green wins as the school's veggie of choice. From the Indian saag paneer to the Greek spanakopita, spinach recipes flooded the newsroom.

In response to new federal regulations that require school lunches to be 63 percent vegetable by weight, The Monitor asked readers to send in their favorite vegetable-based dishes. The Monitor request followed Tuesday's story "Student s Reject, Resent 'Healthy' School Lunches."

The Monitor received more than 80 recipes, a majority of which contained cheese. Click here to see some staff favorites and the most commonly submitted meat-free dish.

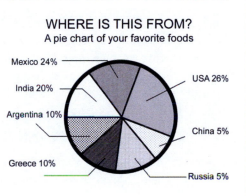

WHERE IS THIS FROM?
A pie chart of your favorite foods

Mexico 24%
India 20%
Argentina 10%
Greece 10%
USA 26%
China 5%
Russia 5%

EXCUSE ME, MS. PICKLES?

YES, DEAR?

I JUST WANTED TO LET YOU KNOW THAT THE ZUCCHINI STEW TODAY WAS *REALLY* GOOD.

THANK YOU, DEAR. I'M JUST LOOKING AT SOME OF THE MEALS YOU KIDS PUBLISHED IN YOUR NEWSPAPER. I DON'T KNOW IF I CAN GET *PLANTAINS* HERE, BUT SOME OF THESE DISHES LOOK REALLY INTERESTING.

OH GOOD, YEAH, WE THOUGHT IT MIGHT HELP YOU TO SEE WHAT WE ARE *ALREADY* EATING.

DO YOU THINK THE SCHOOL DISTRICT WILL LET YOU MAKE ANY OF THOSE?

I DON'T KNOW, BUT IT'S WORTH A SHOT. I JUST NEED TO FIGURE OUT THE COST AND NUTRITIONAL ANALYSIS BEFORE I MEET THEM.

WELL, *GOOD LUCK*, MS. P!

THANKS, DEAR.

Say Cheese!

Photojournalism requires different standards of photo taking than what you share on social media. The goal online is aesthetic. With journalism, the goal is authenticity.

On most basic level, photojournalism is telling a story with images. But even stories told by images need to follow these two rules:

1. Images must be authentic. Photos should not be contrived or posed in a way that makes it looks candid—unless it is indicated as such in the caption.
2. Don't manipulate the reader. Photos should not be edited or cropped in a way that changes the meaning of the original photograph. These techniques can be used to simplify the composition or to direct the reader's eye to an appropriate element but the image itself cannot be altered.

Here are some tips for taking good photos:

- Fill the frame. Whether you are taking a wide, medium, or tight shot, make sure everything within the frame tells the story. Aim for one dominant item per image. This will create a center of interest for the viewer.
- Organize elements. Use the rule of thirds to create pleasing sense of proportion.
- Keep it simple. Fewer elements make a stronger statement.
- Shoot verbs, not nouns. You want some sort of action in your photo, not a still life.
- Include people in photos. Readers respond to faces and emotion in photos.
- If you are using a digital camera, take 90 percent more pictures than you need. If you are planning on submitting five photos to your editor, shoot 50.
- Change it up. Shoot a variety of angles and perspectives. Go high! Go low! Go wide! Go Tight! You'll turn in your best photos so you want to have a variety from which to choose.

Techniques to Use

Just as you want a reader to take in the whole article, you want to frame the photo in a way that the elements guide the viewer's eye through the entire image.

Rule of Thirds

The basic philosophy here is that you don't want the dominant item to be centered in the frame because that's boring. Create a strong focal point by shifting the image off-center. Some cameras allow you to see a tic-tac-toe grid in the viewfinder. Use this to put the focal point of your image in one of the cross points of the grid.

Framing and Crosslines

Use natural elements to highlight the dominant element.

Vantage point

Experiment with shooting from different angles.

Use patterns

A variety of textures and repetition of shapes can make an image come alive.

Play with reflection and shadow

Use light and shadow to capture an unusual image.

Shooting Perspective

Wide shot

These are great shots for setting the scene. It will give the viewer an overall impression of the event or where it took place. This is a good perspective for showing the scope of a rally or sporting event.

Medium shot

This perspective tells the story in a single image. An image of a water pipe break story might have a tearful student in the foreground and city workers battling the deluge in the background. Or for a classic sports shot, a dominant image of a player scoring with the crowd watching in awe.

Close-up or tight shot

You've got to get pretty close to capture an effective close-up that has emotion and interest. Zooming only gets you so far. Aim for making a detail take up a majority of the frame.

Caption Writing

A picture might tell a thousand words but that doesn't mean you don't have to tell the reader what is going on in the picture. The words that accompany a picture is called a caption (or a cutline—each newsroom uses its own terminology).

The goal of the caption is to tell the reader what is happening in the picture. It's a good place to use journalism's favorite question starters: Who, what, where, how and why. Here are some examples:

> Junior Sammi Rahid prefers getting his lunch from Pizza Pete's than from the school cafeteria because "it's tastier."

Makes sure that your caption doesn't state the obvious. In this case you wouldn't write, "Students eat pizza at Pizza Pete's"—that doesn't add anything to the reader's understanding of what is going on in the photo or how it relates to the story.

And just like you want to avoid writing "when asked" in your news stories, avoid writing "pictured here" in your captions.

Not all stories need to have photos and not all photos need to have stories. Feel free to run a standalone photo with a caption. Some news organizations call such illustrations "floaters" or "wild art." This is one way to showcase the work of a great photographer on staff or just to highlight a nice moment at your school. Depending on the topic, these captions can run a little longer, if they need to.

1-2-3 Smile!

If you have to do a posed photo, try to make it less static by including a prop that will tell the reader something relevant about the story. If you're shooting a teacher who races cars, take a photo of the teacher with his or her medals.

The Journalistic Takeaway: Challenge Your Creativity

Be helpful instead of critical.

The Hallway Monitor didn't publish an investigative piece about food waste at the school. Nor did it run a scathing editorial about how bad the new school lunches are. What's the news value in writing about kids not liking school lunch? There is none. Instead, it published a piece that was creative, positive and gave the school with suggestions for improvement.

It can be easy for student journalists to resort to negative coverage, to reflect the lack of influence they feel in how the school operates. However, many administrators see this type coverage as complaining, which isn't proactive. If students focus on providing practical solutions, it's easier for the school to make changes to accommodate the preferences of the student body.

Let's get visual.

Providing data in a visual format is a great way to give readers complex information at a glance. Graphs and charts can save you from trying to write gracefully about numbers, which can often be a challenge. It wasn't critical for the readers of Lolinda's story to see the places of origin for the recipes submitted, but the pie chart was a fun, creative way to draw the reader in.

Maps are another visually interactive way to give readers information that enhances a story. Stories that might benefit from the inclusion of maps include a piece about where seniors are going to college, or about popular vacation spots for teachers and students.

There are free online tools that will guide you in the process of choosing appropriate graphics for your work. Before you consult the internet, ask yourself: What's the single message you want the graphic to convey? From there you will need to figure out the relationship between the data points that you are showing: Are you comparing information or showing locations? This will help you figure out the best format for your data visualization.

The Story Behind the Story: Solution-Based Journalism

One reason journalists love their jobs is because their work can have influence. If they don't cover a story, there is no guarantee someone else will. And that story could have save a life. Matt Richtel wrote 16 articles for *The New York Times* for a series called "Driven to Distraction." The series covered the topic of driving while distracted from a variety of angles: policy, technology, workforce culture, neurologic research, and efforts at prevention. Richtel won a Pulitzer Prize for the series, which resulted in 200 proposed laws throughout the country for limiting the use of cellphones in cars.

There is no way to measure how many lives these laws saved, but they have helped changed public opinion and behavior and create a safer society. And it all started with what Richtel called "asking a good dumb question" about what happens when we turn our cars into offices, where our phones become our computers and messaging centers.

The idea of reporting on effective fixes to a community problem is a trend within the industry known as solutions journalism. The goal of journalism isn't to always report on things that are wrong or bad. It's to help move the conversation productively forward.

For example, in 2015 *The Seattle Times* Education Lab ran on story about a community truancy board program in eastern Washington. Less than two years later, the state legislature made it mandatory for every school district to implement a similar program. The legislature knew about the program, but the public pressure after the story came out led to this new legislation.

While it wasn't specifically solutions-based journalism, *The Hallway Monitor* served its readers well in its coverage of the cafeteria lunch crisis. Instead of focusing on uneaten lunches, they bypassed the negativity and solved the issue with creativity and audience involvement.

Classroom Activities

News Writing

Rewrite the following sentences so they have fewer words.

SAMPLE:

Audience members were relentless with asking the tough questions, including some questions about the panelists' legal records. [17 words]

Audience members asked tough questions about the panelists' legal records. [10 words]

1. Human emissions of heat-trapping gases have begun melting our planet's glaciers. [11 words]
2. Activists protested at a demonstration in June 2016 to protest a bill that would establish $3 billion in cuts to Medicaid. [21 words]
3. High school students can suffer from both stress and anxiety just from the sheer amount of homework teachers give them, causing their mental health humbers to go up in the last few years. [33 words]
4. Maxwell High should be providing ways for students to have access to computers because of the number of homework assignments we get that require computer usage. [26 words]
5. Flores took action by going to her assistant principal to talk about the inaccessibility at her high school. [18 words]

Shot Lists

A shot list describes the photos you want to accompany a story. Creating a shot list is a little like writing your interview questions in advance: It helps you plan the best way to illustrate a story.

For each of the headlines, write down five photos that you think would work well with the article.

SAMPLE:

- Water Fountains Busted on Third Floor
  1. *3rd floor fountain with "Do not use" sign*
  2. *students lining up to use fountains on 1st or 2nd floor*
  3. *students buying water at local store*
  4. *empty water bottle on the lab table on the 3rd floor*
  5. *custodians repairing busted fountains*

- Wrestlers Bulk Up for State Competition
- Benches Brighten Courtyard
- District Approves School Budget

Show, Don't Tell

Use your imagination to rewrite these sentences so they focus on descriptive facts.

<u>SAMPLE:</u>

The online magazine covers everything from art to sports.

Last week's edition featured everything from "The Short and Wondrous Life of Basquiat" to "Lacrosse Players Protests New Field Trip Rules."

1. Mikal Simonov was a true leader that day.
2. She was really involved at her temple.
3. The whole group worked tirelessly to meet their goal.
4. When she first started junior high, Julia Gonzalez noticed that there were many places in the school that she didn't have access to in her wheelchair.
5. It's been years since the newspaper staff tackled tough topics.

Chapter 5:

FOLLOW THE SHUTTLECOCK

THE VALUE OF INDEPENDENT SOURCES

How to Stay Out of Trouble

Journalism is one of the only professions referred to in the U.S. Constitution. This gives reporters a special role in society that is accompanied by a high level of responsibility. Journalists can get in serious trouble if they don't follow legal and ethical guidelines.

As a student journalist, it's important to observe the following rules

1. Don't publish rumors. Journalism is a craft based on verification. You need direct proof that something is true before you can publish it.
2. Don't publish other people's photos and artwork without their permission. Giving credit isn't enough. See more on "How to Avoid Copyright Infringement," on the next page.
3. Verify that all quotations are accurate. Just because a city council member said her opponent lives outside district lines, doesn't make it true.
4. Know what libel is and how to avoid it.
5. Don't break the law or invade someone's privacy.
6. Beware of burning a source by publishing a name after promising anonymity.
7. Every article credited to you must be factual and written by you. Fabrication and plagiarism and are the cardinal sins of journalism.

What is libel?

Libel is the publication of a false statement that deliberately or carelessly damages someone's reputation. A libel case is based on the following criteria:

1. It must be false
2. It must be defamatory
3. It must be published
4. The plaintiff must be identifiable
5. The defendant must be at fault

Avoiding libel

✗ "Students say local hairdresser Layne Stephens is always running behind during prom season. A 30 minute blow-out can turn into a 90-minute appointment, wreaking havoc on promgoers schedule."

- This account is potentially libelous. No evidence is given and it doesn't include a response from Stephens.

✓ "Students say some hairdressers are slammed during prom season. Last year, Teresa Whitman's 30 minute blow-out turned into a 90-minute appointment, wreaking havoc on her prom day schedule."

- This account avoids libel by not mentioning a specific hairdresser.

How to Avoid Copyright Infringement

Most student journalists don't intentionally pilfer the creative work of someone else, they just don't know the rules.

Here are the rules

Contrary to popular belief, using an image from the internet is a violation of copyright, even if you give the owner credit. Don't be a thief. Instead, use art that is in the public domain or has a Creative Commons license.

What is a Creative Commons license?

A Creative Commons license is an alternative to a copyright. It allows others to use an image or a song or the product of someone else's creativity for free with appropriate credit. There are different types of CC licenses. Some apply only to commercial entities, others only for noncommercial purposes.

This license indicates you may use an image "as is."	This license indicates the image can be revised.
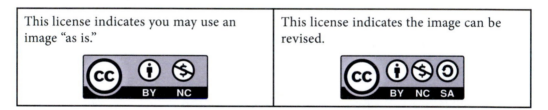	

For further information, visit: **https://creativecommons.org/licenses/**

It's a requirement of all Creative Commons licenses that you attribute the original author. This means you can't just use a creative commons image without acknowledging the person who originally created it. Within or next to the usage, you must give attribution and you must link the photo back to its original photo page.

Credit: orphanjoneson Flickr, via Creative Commons https://www.flickr.com/photos/orphanjones/402444634/sizes/l

What's in the public domain?

When something isn't covered by copyright, because it never had one or because it expired, it's consider to be in the public domain, which means it is free to use. Most government images and images that are super old (published before 1923) are usually, but not always, in the public domain. Cornell University provides a detailed guide to copyright terms and public domain on their website.

If you want to reproduce material, but are unsure of the copyright status a good general rule of thumb is: When in doubt, ask for permission. If you don't get a response, don't use the content.

But wait!

There is an exception, of course. Fair use is a principle of copyright law that permits reproduction of a small portion of a copyrighted work in another work. For example, a quotation from a book, or the use of a photograph that complements the new work. There are a number of factors that are taken into consideration in determining fair use, including the proportion of content being used and how its reproduction might impact the sale of the original source. For example, you can publish an image of a book cover to supplement a review, and perhaps incorporate a few brief quotations that serve to highlight points made in the review, but more extensive use would require permission from the publisher. Remember, company logos count as art and can only be used if the company is relevant to the article it appears in. You can't use the Apple logo on the cover your yearbook, just because you think it looks cool.

Check Chapter 10 for a list of places online where you can find free and legal images and music to use in your newspapers, websites, and broadcasts.

Make Your Opinion Count

Editorials and op-eds are two of the most popular types of articles for students to write, but they are also among the most difficult to do correctly.

What's the difference between an Editorial and an Op-Ed?

Editorials are unsigned (no byline) articles produced by editorial staff of a publication. Opinion pieces (also called op-eds) have a byline and are traditionally (in the professional world) written by someone not on staff at the newspaper.

Both have a similar goal in mind: To share a perspective or a view, in order to change someone's mind or affect a process. The best way to do this is not to tell the reader what you think. Instead, tell them why the status quo isn't working. Present them with a true (not hypothetical) situation that exemplifies what's wrong with how things are going now. Then use that as an opportunity to share your suggestions for improvement or your view of the situation.

Keep your editorial or opinion piece short. You should be able to say what you need to say in 500 words or less. If you can't, rethink your argument and rewrite. You don't want your article to be a rant. You want it to be clear and concise. Here is a simple way to set-up your piece:

1. Share an anecdote that illustrates the problem.
2. Explain what the current process is for dealing with the issue.
3. Tell the reader what the pitfalls or challenges to the current solution are.
4. Disclose your suggestion on what should happen.
5. Demonstrate why your idea is better than the one in action now.
6. End with a firm sentence that gets the point across of how important this topic is.

Editorials are typically shorter than opinion articles. If that is the case in your publication, you can skip the anecdote and jump straight into the proposed solution for the existing problem.

"Op-eds" are opinion pieces. They are called op-eds because they traditionally appear opposite the editorial page.

NOTE: Even though these are popular pieces, be careful not to fill the paper with op-eds. Everyone wants to sound off, but reporting is more valuable. And even editorials and opinion pieces require reporting!

KUBBLE'S SOURCE LIST

"FUNDRAISING BEGINS FOR $70 million BADMINTON COURT"

- PRINCIPAL EVENS
- SOMEONE FROM THE SCHOOL BOARD
- ALUMNI CHAIR
- STUDENT ATHLETES
- STUDENT COUNCIL
- NATIONAL BADMINTON ASSOCIATION
- THE INITIAL FUNDRAISING LETTER EVANS SENT OUT
- CENTERS FOR DISEASE CONTROL AND PREVENTION

"PRINCIPAL MISLEAD DONORS IN FUNDRAISING CAMPAIGN"

- NATIONAL BADMINTON ASSOCIATION
- ARCHIVAL NEWS ARTICLES
- SCHOOL BOARD
- ALUMNI CHAIR
- DISTRICT SUPERINTENDENT
- STUDENTS
- PRINCIPAL EVENS
- DONORS
- CORPORATE SPONSORS
- DISTRICT PUBLIC RELATIONS SPOKEPERSON

"EVANS RETURNS MONEY TO DONORS"

- SCHOOL BOARD
- ALUMNI CHAIR
- DISTRICT SUPERINTENDENT
- STUDENTS
- PRINCIPAL EVENS
- DONORS
- DISTRICT P.R. SPOKEPERSON
- LETTER TO DONORS

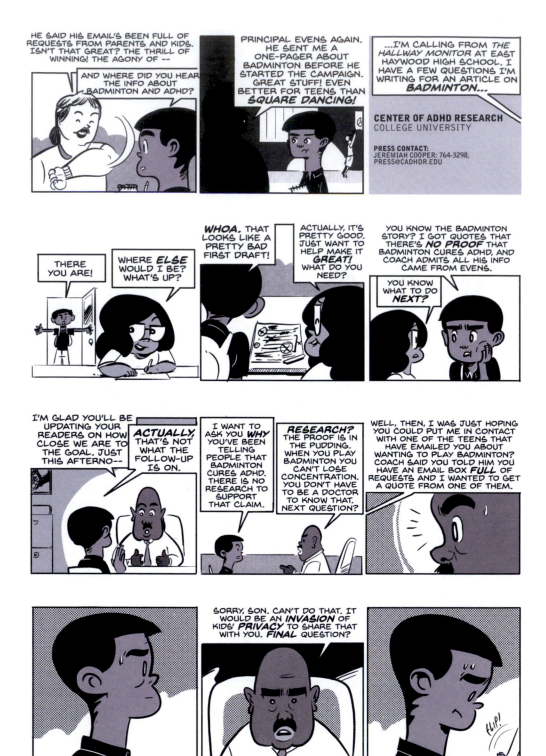

Using Data in News Stories

Data—numbers, statistics, percentages—can often make the difference between a pretty good news story and a truly excellent one. Here are some basic rules for using data in stories:

The best source of data is your own reporting.

Do your own poll, survey or count if possible.

If you don't generate the data yourself, the most reliable data comes from the origin of the information (primary source).

If the information is from a government study, look at the actual report, not a newspaper article about the report. Let's say you find a statistic on the local child welfare agency's website about the number of homeless children in the country. You have to find out if the agency did the research themselves or are they quoting another source. How do you find out?

Look carefully on its site for the source of the data. If it is not listed, you have to contact the agency and found out. While you're at it, find out the date of the research. If more than five years old, find something more recent.

Put the data into context.

A number doesn't mean anything without its context. Has the number increased or decreased? How does it compare to other numbers?

Beware of false comparisons.

Make sure to compare apples with apples.

Be transparent.

Always cite the source of your data.

Read the example below from an article in *The New York Times* on May 12, 2012 about a large increase in the amount of debt that students are racking up to get through college ("Degrees of Debt" by Andrew Martin and Andrew W. Lehren) and see how the citation of a primary source and context change the credibility of the information:

"Most students who earn a bachelor's degree borrow to pay for higher education." (True, of course, but we all pretty much knew that.)

"Ninety-four percent of students who earn a bachelor's degree borrow to pay for higher education..." (That's almost all college students. But has it always been this way? How much has the number of students in debt increased? The sentence lacks context.)

"Ninety-four percent of students who earn a bachelor's degree borrow to pay for higher education—up from 45 percent in 1993..." (Better, but still raises a question for the reader: where is this information from and how do we know we can trust it?)

This is how the sentence ran in The New York Times:

"Ninety-four percent of students who earn a bachelor's degree borrow to pay for higher education—up from 45 percent in 1993, according to an analysis by The New York Times of the latest data from the Department of Education." (It's just one simple sentence, but it anchors the whole story.)

The Journalistic Takeaway: You Can't Always Believe What People Tell You

Just because a source said it doesn't make it true.

Your job as a reporter is to find out and publish the truth, not just what people tell you. Journalism requires verification. You need to provide proof for everything you write. In Kubble's case, he was skeptical about the information he received from Principal Evens but he published it anyway. If you don't believe your source, why should the reader? Even if Kubble didn't have doubts, he should have researched the connection between ADHD and badminton before he published the story.

Consult an expert as an outside source to put the situation in context.

What you're looking for from this **Voice of Authority** is someone with professional expertise on the issue. Experts can do more than provide verification. They also offer context and because they are not directly involved, they can provide a bird's eye view of the situation, which helps the reader see your story as part of a larger issue. Prepare a separate set of questions for this source.

Don't be afraid of a follow-up interview.

Just because you talked to a source once, don't feel like you can't go back with follow-up questions. Your source won't be annoyed. In fact, he or she will be happy that you're being diligent about getting the facts straight. And if they are annoyed, you can explain that you're coming back because you care so much about accuracy.

The need for a follow-up interview often pops up once you start writing your article. You (or your editor) may realize you need information you don't have. This is a good time to go back to the source because you can ask specific questions that fill in a blank in your story. Expect these interviews to be shorter and more casual.

In some cases you'll have to ask your source for evidence—just like Kubble did to get proof of students' interest in badminton. When your source can't provide proof that something he or she said is true, proceed with caution.

The Story Behind the Story:
Words Can be Weapons
of Mass Destruction

A lot can ride on what a journalist writes. Judith Miller's reporting on weapons of mass destruction contributed to the American invasion of Iraq in 2003. She wrote a series of articles for *The New York Times* where she claimed that Iraq had secret biological and chemical weapons. The problem? Her reporting was based on a single source with a sketchy reputation. Unbeknownst to her, the source was providing information secretly to the same intelligence committee that she was reporting on. *The New York Times* Public Editor eventually described the information as "the anonymity-cloaked assertions of people with vested interests."

The impact of this story was huge. It "provided the justification the Americans had been seeking for the invasion," *The Times* wrote in an editor's note. But, as they "never followed up on the veracity of this source or the attempts to verify his claims," *The Times* contributed to false justification for war.

Miller, a Pulitzer Prize-winning journalist, responded that she was only reporting on what she was told and she, like the government agency, was a victim of misinformation. Without independent verification no one discovered that Miller's source was lying. The belief in the existence of WMD was the tipping point that got the U.S. involved in the war, which has caused more than 6,000 civilian casualties, *The Guardian* reports.

Miller admitted to making mistakes in her reporting on Iraq. "I wish I could have interviewed senior officials before the war about the role that WMDs played in the decision to invade Iraq," she wrote in *The Wall Street Journal* in 2015. "The White House's passion for secrecy and aversion to the media made that unlikely."

Of course the issue goes beyond one reporter. In its own coverage, *The Times* called the root of the problem "complicated." "Editors at several levels who should have been challenging reporters and pressing for more skepticism were perhaps too intent on rushing scoops into the paper," an editor's note stated.

You can read a full assessment of the situation on the *American Journalism Review* website under "Miller Brouhaha."

Classroom Activities

Charting Your Reporting Path

Where or to whom would you go to find the following information about your school?

1. The total number of female and male students in your school

2. The vote count in the last student council election

3. How much the last school dance cost, and how it was funded

4. How much the school cafeteria has to spend per student on lunch every day

5. The percentage of last year's graduating class who went to college right after high school

6. What questions are you curious to find out the answers to about your school?

7. Choose one of these questions and find out the answer. Explain how you got the information, or your reporting trail.

Perspectives with a Punch

Read the below editorial from *The Southwest Shadow* and then identify these parts by underlining the section and marking with the associated letter.

A. An anecdote that illustrates the problem

B. The current process for dealing with the issue

C. Problems with the current solution

D. The fresh perspective

E. The benefits of the writer's suggestion

EDITORIAL: Mandatory AP testing for GPA bump sets poor precedent for students

GPA bump is earned even for a failed exam

Drafting his ideal class schedule for next year, senior Hassan Bhatti hesitates. Four AP classes or three? He thinks back to the rumors circulating around school from teachers and students: *"All AP tests are mandatory for the upcoming school year. But as long as you take it, you'll get the AP GPA bump for your classes."*

Four, he decides.

During the 2015–2016 school year, Clark County School District mandated that AP students had to take each $93 exam for any AP classes taken in order to gain the AP GPA incentive increase of 0.050. If the test is not taken, students will gain an Honors GPA increase of only 0.025 points.

93

Prior to this decision, all students, regardless of whether or not they decided to take the test, were able to gain the 0.050 GPA increase. This decision has a debilitating effect on students and their AP class enrollment. They may now feel discouraged from taking AP classes for fear of having to pay for exams they may not pass.

Additionally, students may not opt out of taking the tests themselves; only parents may give their child written permission to do so. This means that students are left to plead with their parents to either potentially break the bank now or to let them skip a test that could earn the student college credit and save the family money down the road.

While the methods for how the test costs will be covered has not been announced, it is assumed that all but low-income students must pay the full price for each AP test they take. Students eligible for free or reduced lunch will only be charged $15 per test. The recent mandate means thousands of Nevada students will have to pay up to $279 for three AP exams if they wish to receive the GPA increase they were expecting. This means students will be left on their own to foot the bill for up to three tests they may not feel prepared for—or miss out on a GPA bump they would have rightfully earned otherwise.

For students like Bhatti, who is taking four AP classes, this is concerning news.

"I enjoy taking AP classes because they are challenging. I decided to take as many as I could while still having a relatively low-stress year," Bhatti said. "If a student isn't prepared to take the test, they shouldn't be forced to. Making AP tests mandatory is simply scaring students and preventing them from challenging themselves."

In other areas of Nevada, such as Washoe County School District, AP tests have been mandatory for years. This establishes a precedent where all students are aware and prepared to pay for the exams they are required to take. Students in CCSD do not have this luxury, however, as the district failed to broadcast its final decision to make AP testing mandatory. There were no press releases or news articles from the district regarding the major change and some students are still unaware of the change.

In order to amend the unmet expectations CCSD put forth the district should work with schools in the valley to attempt to alleviate costs for all students, as well as reconsider the mandating of AP tests for next year.

"It's like they're saying, 'Oh that student is challenging him/herself, we shouldn't give them credit for doing so,'" Bhatti said. "People really don't understand the effort AP students put in, and then they get treated like this."

Used with permission of The Southwest Shadow *at Southwest Career and Technical Academy (Las Vegas).*

Outline your own perspective piece

Topic:

- What is the problem?
- What is the current solution?
- Why doesn't the current solution work?
- What anecdote will you use to illustrate the faults in the current approach?

- What is your idea for fixing the problem?
- Why would this idea work where the current one has failed?

Using the guides in Chapter 10, find three copyright-free photos to illustrate these headlines

- Students Misled by Asbestos Signs on Campus
- Art Squad Draws New Chapter
- New Make-Up Rules Rankle Student Athletes
- Internet Security Evades Students

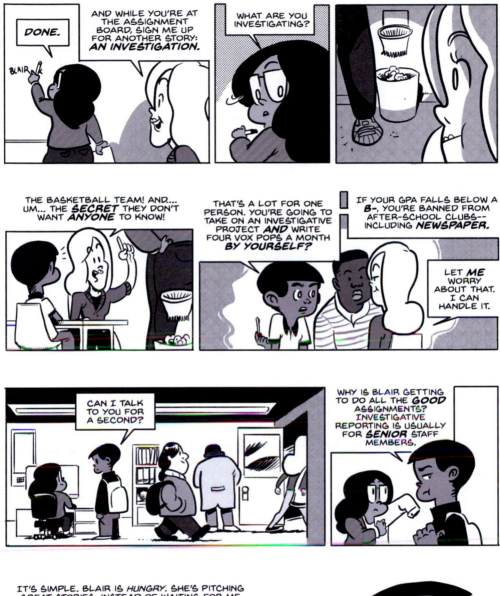

DONE.

BLAIR

AND WHILE YOU'RE AT THE ASSIGNMENT BOARD, SIGN ME UP FOR ANOTHER STORY: *AN INVESTIGATION.*

WHAT ARE YOU INVESTIGATING?

THE BASKETBALL TEAM! AND.... UM... THE *SECRET* THEY DON'T WANT *ANYONE* TO KNOW!

THAT'S A LOT FOR ONE PERSON. YOU'RE GOING TO TAKE ON AN INVESTIGATIVE PROJECT *AND* WRITE FOUR VOX POPS A MONTH *BY YOURSELF?*

IF YOUR GPA FALLS BELOW A *B-*, YOU'RE BANNED FROM AFTER-SCHOOL CLUBS-- INCLUDING *NEWSPAPER.*

LET *ME* WORRY ABOUT THAT. I CAN HANDLE IT.

CAN I TALK TO YOU FOR A SECOND?

WHY IS BLAIR GETTING TO DO ALL THE *GOOD* ASSIGNMENTS? INVESTIGATIVE REPORTING IS USUALLY FOR *SENIOR* STAFF MEMBERS.

IT'S SIMPLE. BLAIR IS *HUNGRY.* SHE'S PITCHING GREAT STORIES, INSTEAD OF WAITING FOR ME TO HAND HER AN ASSIGNMENT. PLUS, SHE MEETS HER DEADLINES AND DOESN'T COMPLAIN. HER COPY IS CLEAN AND HER REPORTING IS SOLID. SHE'S *THAT GOOD.*

NO ONE'S *THAT* GOOD.

Copy Flow

How does a story idea become an article? Every news-room has a different process, but generally it involves a lot of communication between staffers and multiple revisions from the writer. The key to keeping the process on track is meeting deadlines. Your editor would rather have a draft on time with a few holes, than late and complete. In news, timing is everything.

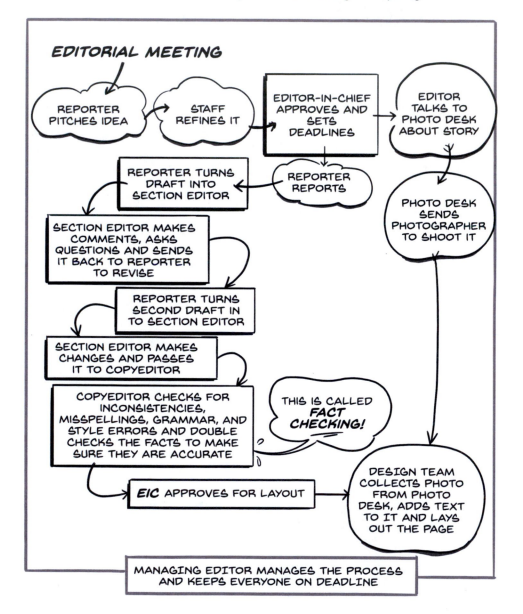

EDITORIAL MEETING

REPORTER PITCHES IDEA → STAFF REFINES IT → EDITOR-IN-CHIEF APPROVES AND SETS DEADLINES → EDITOR TALKS TO PHOTO DESK ABOUT STORY

REPORTER TURNS DRAFT INTO SECTION EDITOR ← REPORTER REPORTS

PHOTO DESK SENDS PHOTOGRAPHER TO SHOOT IT

SECTION EDITOR MAKES COMMENTS, ASKS QUESTIONS AND SENDS IT BACK TO REPORTER TO REVISE

REPORTER TURNS SECOND DRAFT IN TO SECTION EDITOR

SECTION EDITOR MAKES CHANGES AND PASSES IT TO COPYEDITOR

COPYEDITOR CHECKS FOR INCONSISTENCIES, MISSPELLINGS, GRAMMAR, AND STYLE ERRORS AND DOUBLE CHECKS THE FACTS TO MAKE SURE THEY ARE ACCURATE

THIS IS CALLED *FACT CHECKING!*

EIC APPROVES FOR LAYOUT

DESIGN TEAM COLLECTS PHOTO FROM PHOTO DESK, ADDS TEXT TO IT AND LAYS OUT THE PAGE

MANAGING EDITOR MANAGES THE PROCESS AND KEEPS EVERYONE ON DEADLINE

Editorial Checklist

What is Blair's editor looking for when reading her story? She's making sure her news article follows the tenets of good journalism. Here's what editors and copy editors should be alert to when reviewing an article.

Uses an Objective Perspective

☐ Are any of these words used in the news or feature article, with the exception of quoted material: I, you, me, we, us, our, your, etc.?

☐ Do any words indicate how the writer feels about the topic?

☐ Does the writer avoid cheerleading for the school?

Provides Multiple Independent Sources and Is Fair

☐ Are there at least three independent sources in the article?

☐ Does the article contain at least three quotations from different sources?

☐ For an article on a controversial subject, does it include fair representation of opposing viewpoints?

☐ Were all relevant segments of the high school community (administrators, teachers, staff) given a chance to respond?

Relies on Original Reporting

☐ Can you find anything in the story that seems like a generalization?

☐ Is the article substantially reported by the student journalists as opposed to repeating previously published material?

☐ Have experts—either in-school or outside of school—been interviewed?

Limits Anonymous Sources

☐ Does the writer use anonymous sources?

☐ If so, are the reasons spelled out in the story?

Statistics Are Nonpartisan

☐ When results from polls or surveys are used, does the article state when, where, how, and by whom the poll was conducted?

☐ Does it report how many were polled?

☐ Does all data come from reputable sources?

Note: See Chapter 10 for "Use of Sources: A Checklist for Reporters & Editors."

Fact Checking

If *The Hallway Monitor* had a fact-checker, here are some things the staffer might have marked on Blair's basketball story.

Foul! Grizzlies Are in a Real (Toe) Jam This Time

By Blair Jayson

A new menace is lurking in the boy's locker room, in the tiles of the showers and the oors beneath the lockers – athlete's foot.

GREAT QUOTE. ALMOST TOO GREAT. IS IT FOR REAL?

"It started with an itchy feeling under my sweat socks," said one junior varsity team member, who did not want his name used. "Then my toes started itching like crazy. I pulled my sock off and a shower of skin flaked off the bottom of my foot."

ANONYMOUS QUOTE!

Before long, seven of the eight players on the varsity basketball team and eight of the 12 players on junior varsity had come down with athlete's foot.

WHAT IS THE SOURCE OF THIS INFO?

Athlete's foot (also known as ringworm of the foot and Tinea pedis) is a fungal infection of the skin that causes scaling, aking, and itch of affected areas. It is caused by fungi in the genus Trichophyton and is typically transmitted in moist areas where people walk barefoot, such as showers or bathhouses. Although the condition typically affects the feet, it can spread to other areas of the body, including the groin. Athlete's foot can be treated by a number of pharmaceuticals (including creams) and other treatments.

THE STYLE OF THIS GRAF IS A BIG SHIFT – SEARCH ONLINE FOR PHRASES. (FOUND ON WIKIPEDIA.)

"Eew," said Sarah Snifter, when told about the outbreak. "And I heard this isn't the first fungal infection that the basketball team has had. Last year there were rumors of a jock itch epidemic!"

UNSUBSTANTIATED RUMOR.

As of yesterday, there were no reports of athlete's foot infections in the girls' locker room. But with only about 30 feet between the boys' and girls' locker room the infection is likely to jump from one to another.

UNFOUNDED SPECULATION.

In addition to looking for items that might be suspect, you want to fact check for correct spellings and accurate information. Sometimes you can use the Internet to help you verify details other times you'll have to go back to the source.

Let's say the article says someone's title is director but the staff page for the organization online lists this person as "Youth Director." Did the person get a promotion, which the staff page has yet to update or did the reporter write down the information incorrectly? It's always good to get information you find online verified by an official source. Whether it is somebody's title or the date of an upcoming event, information changes frequently and you can't always trust that a website is up to date.

Here are items in an article that you will want to fact check before publication:

Names of people, cities, schools: Are they spelled right? "Michele" or "Michelle"; "Brooklyn" or "Brooklin"

Titles: Very few people actually have the title "Chief Cook and Bottle Washer" so it's your job to find out their official title.

Hyperlinks and urls: Do links work and do they lead you to the original source of the information (not to a news report about the research)?

Research findings: Is the writer's summary of the research correct?

Dates: Was Tinker v. Des Moines in 1967 or 1969? Check all dates.

Numbers: Anything with a number is good to double check.

Rankings: Is Bill Gates the richest man in the world or is Jeff Bezos?

Information provided by others: If a neighbor tells you his asthma is due to the rising sea levels, you have to be responsible for the information and see if there is any research that higher sea levels affect asthma rates.

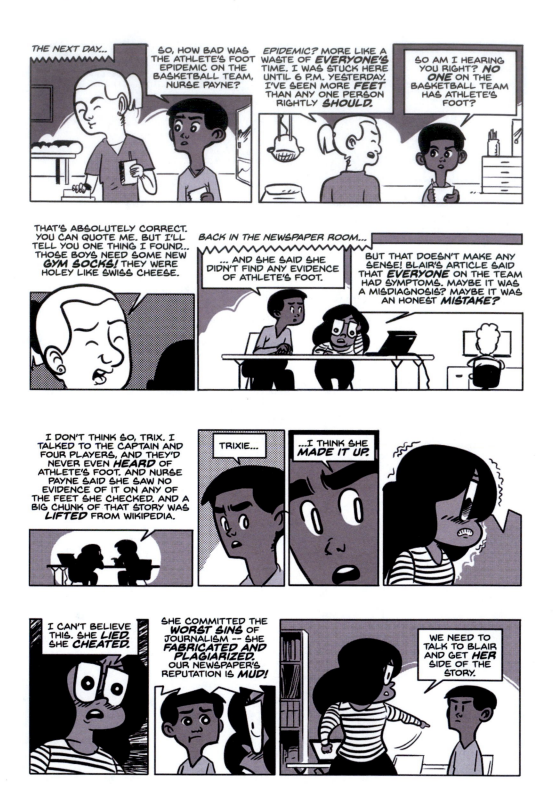

What Is Plagiarism?

When writers use material from other sources, they must make it clear that it is not their original work and specifically mention the source. Not doing so is called plagiarism, which means using, without credit, the ideas or expressions of another.

This applies to the work of other students as well as the published work of professional writers. Of course, this also applies to information you find on the Internet or other digital sources.

Plagiarism Is a Serious Academic Offense and Includes:

1. Using, word for word, phrases, sentences, paragraphs, etc., from the writing of others without making it clear that you are using another's writing or ideas.
2. Using the materials of another with slight changes.
3. Using the general plan, the main headings, or a rewritten form of someone else's material.

(adapted from an article written by Professor Irwin Weiser of Purdue University)

In *The New York Times*, writer Kelefa Sanneh describes Keyshia Cole's new album, *Just Like You*, as a "likeable and well-sung album." ◄—— **Citing:** For some of your assignments, you may do research in books, newspapers, magazines, or on the Internet, but it is extremely important that you "cite" these sources. To "cite" something means to give credit to the original source of the material.

"There's plenty of heartbreak here," *The New York Times* writer Kelefa Sanneh wrote of Keyshia Cole's new album, *Just Like You*. In his review of the album, Sanneh argues that Cole "prefers breakup songs to hook-up songs." ◄—— **Quoting:** When you are using the exact words of another writer, you must put them in quote marks and be very clear about whose words they are.

Keisha Cole's new album, *Just Like You*, is less angry than her first album, but still packs an emotional punch, according to Kelefa Sanneh, a writer for *The New York Times*. ◄—— **Paraphrasing:** When you are explaining a point that another writer made, but using different words to do it, you must still explain the source of the ideas you're expressing.

In newspapers, professional or student, the consequences for plagiarism are severe.
If in doubt, always cite your source, rather than risk plagiarizing.

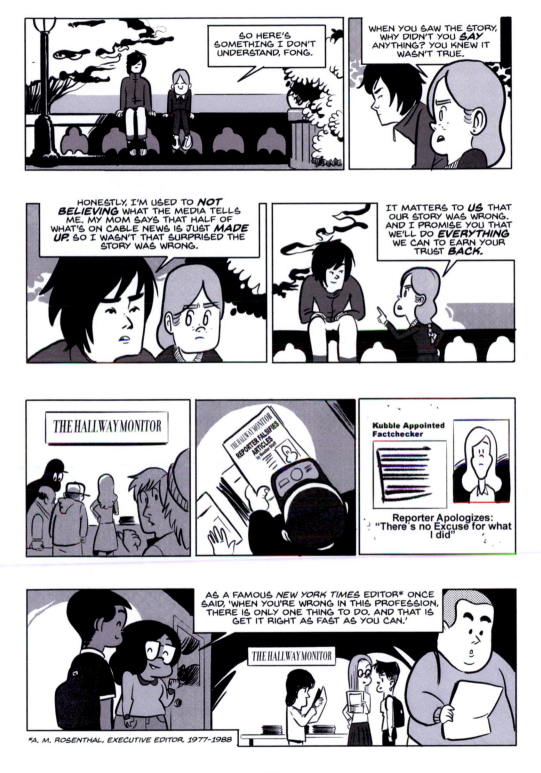

The Journalistic Takeaway: Facts Are Where It's At

Sometimes you feel a lot of pressure to feed the beat, but that's never an excuse to make things up.

What *The Hallway Monitor* is selling to its readers is trust. It's no different from *The Washington Post* or the *Arizona Daily Star*. Newspapers earn this trust by being accurate, relevant, and responsive—and most of all, factual. Blair frayed the bond between *The Hallway Monitor* and its readers with every made up word. Once the truth came out, *The Hallway Monitor* had a responsibility to address the issue publicly.

So what should you do when you're under deadline and you don't have the quotes? Talk to your editor and fess up. Your editor won't be happy, but he would rather lose a story then run the risk of jeopordizing the public trust in journalism.

Love thy fact checker.

Your newspaper is responsible for the information it publishes, whatever the source. A fact checker's role is to double check the reporter's work and make sure information and details are correct. Imagine how bad it would look if your opinion piece on gun laws referred to the 4th Amendment, instead of the 2nd? Erroneous details undermine the credibility of the reporter.

And remember: Just because someone said something—even someone in a position of authority—doesn't make it true. If a source tells you that your school building was a former milk factory, you have to confirm that it was a milk factory and not a fromagerie (cheese shop).

Because newspapers and magazines have been struggling financially in recent years, they don't always have as many fact checkers as before but, that doesn't mean fact checking's not an essential part of journalism.

Transparency is your jam, spread it thick.

Once the truth came out, *The Hallway Monitor* had a responsibility to its readers to explain how such an egregious error was made. By retracing Blair's reporting footsteps, they turned the spotlight on themselves. To make sure the problem never happened again, they had to figure out what went wrong. To make sure their readers know how seriously they took the incident, they made their investigation public and published their findings.

This transparency—letting the public see how journalism works—is key to establishing trust. It is why newspapers should tell readers *why* the paper granted anonymity to a source. Whether the source is undocumented and afraid of deportation or fearful the school administration will retaliate, reporters need to tell the readers the rationale behind the decision.

Another example of transparency is when reporter explains that she tried to reach a key source for comment but never got a reponse. If the journalist had left this out of the story, the reader wouldn't know that she made an attempt to contact that source.

The Story Behind the Story:
Infamous Perpetrators of Plagiarism

Unfortunately there have been many infamous cases where journalistic integrity went out the window.

Jayson Blair: In 2003, *The New York Times* realized one of its most promising young reporters was also its least truthful. When editors discovered that reporter Jayson Blair had plagiarized stories and fabricated quotes, it put together a team of investigative reporters to uncover what happened and who was to blame. The resulting article is a fascinating insight into newsroom politics and personalities.

Here's the thing about Blair: His transgressions started in college. According to U-Wire. com, he falsified quotes a story for his college newspaper *The Diamondback* (University of Maryland, College Park). Makes you wonder when his trail of deception started.

Stephen Glass: With a last name like Glass, don't you think you'd try harder to be transparent? The editors at *The New Republic*, a biweekly news magazine, certainly wish their associate editor Glass lived up to his name. Instead he published an article about computer hackers in the May 18, 1998, issue that was entirely fabricated. How'd this happen? Why did he do it? Watch *Shattered Glass* and find out.

Patricia Smith/Mike Barnicle: The upsides to having a biweekly column are popularity, guaranteed bylines and a strong following of readers. The downsides are deadlines, deadlines, and deadlines. There is a lot of pressure to produce original, thought-provoking reported columns. What happens when that pressure gets too much? Well, in 1998 at *The Boston Globe* two columnists thought they could make up quotes for imaginary people. They lost their jobs and the trust of millions of readers across the country.

Janet Cooke: Janet Cooke is perhaps the most rejected former journalist in newsrooms. In 1981 Cooke won a Pulitzer Prize for an article she wrote for *The Washington Post* about an 8-year-old heroin addict named Jimmy. She pulled on the heartstrings of her readers and galvanized a city into action to protect little Jimmy. Only thing is, Jimmy didn't exist. Two days after she won the Pulitzer—like the Oscar awards of journalism—she confessed, returned the award and resigned from the newspaper. Cooke claimed Jimmy was a composite—a character composed of real characteristics of several real individuals. Composite characters are permissible only when clearly identified upfront for the reader and even then the real thing is often more powerful.

The Village Voice: A few months after New York City's alternative magazine, *The Village Voice*, laid off its fact checking department in 2006, the weekly was threatened with a lawsuit by a screenwriter whose name a reporter used in a fabricated scenario for a story on NYC's dating scene. The writer was suspended and the acting editor in chief stepped down.

Classroom Activities

Fact Checking Boot Camp

1. **In the below passage, underline the items that need to be fact checked.**

   Teens are finding their way around laws in 12 states that make it illegal for anyone under 18 to use indoor tanning facilities. With or without their parents' knowledge some teens are walking into salons and exposing themselves to ultraviolet radiation that can increase their risk of the skin cancer melanoma by 20 percent in just one visit. These increasing reports on these dangers have called for the organizations to classify indoor tanning as "carcinogenic to humans." Federal authorities required tanning machines to list specific warnings for minors, but that doesn't mean all salons are doing their part to keep teens out.

   From "Teen's Love of Illegal Tanning Booths Defies Risks" by Annabel Thorpe
   Teen Voices at Women's eNews

2. **Fact-check the following "Facts."**

"FACT"	True or False	Source
In 2006, the population of St. Paul, Minnesota was 273,535.	True	According to http://quickfacts. census. gov/qfd/states/27/2758 000.html
The 11th Amendment of the Constitution abolished slavery.	False	The 13th Amendment does that. http://www.archives.gov/exhibits/ charters/constitution_ amendments_11–27.html#13
Filipino Americans have the highest rate of asthma in the United States.		
The Soviet Union disbanded in 1992.		
Crayola crayons have been around since 1927.		
Traveling is spelled with lls.		
Twenty-six percent of the US is under 18 years old.		
Tinker vs Board of Education was decided on in 1977.		
Canadian universities had an increase in applications after Nov. 8, 2016.		

3. **Use the editorial checklist to review an article in your student newspaper.**

Pitches

Pitch (n.): In journalism a pitch is a brief description of a story a writer wants to produce.

A good pitch makes it clear to the editor what you want to write about, tells them why it matters and proves you are the right person for job. Even if your editor doesn't require one, a pitch helps you organize your thoughts, even before you start reporting.

First, understand the difference between a topic and pitch. Saying, "I want to write about drones" merely states your topic. Specifying, "I want to write about the recent donation of a drone to the robotics club" transforms your topic into a pitch.

Questions you want to answer in your pitch:

1. What's happening now that wasn't happening before? (What's the news?)
2. Why do you want to tell this story now?
3. Why does it matter?
4. Who will you talk to for your story and what will you find out from them?

Second, make sure the pitch is directly related to the publication's audience. Remember, every story should have a direct tie to your school community.

Third, do your research.

Look for statistics and research why this is an important story. Make sure the information is recent. You can pull from pop culture or current events to show why this article will be widely read.

Check out these two pitches for the drone story:

The robotics club got a new drone. This article will cover how the members are enjoying the new toy and how they hope to learn from it. Lots of people have drones so it is good that the members of the club will know how to use them. Plus it will help them win competitions against richer schools.	The robotics club was recently given a drone by an alumni of the school. This article will cover club plans to use the drone and how it will enable them to participate in state-level competitions. I will talk to the club president, a club member, and the person who donated the drone. I will also look into how drone usage has become a part of recent robotic competitions. Last year, more than two million drones were sold nationally, double the previous year. As the technology improves, the drone market will increase, along with the need for training in their production and use.

Both pitches are similar but the one on the right is more thorough and and demonstrates that the writer did some research beforehand. It is also more objective.

Food Writing

Food writing is a great way to explore the various cultures represented by students, and give them the opportunity to share family stories. Everybody eats, so writing about food can be appreciated on both a personal and universal level.

Here are some ideas

Trend stories: What ingredient is suddenly popping up everywhere? Is there a beverage your student body can't get enough of right now? **Food trend stories help show your readers you are in tune with them.** The angle could be straightforward: where did it start and why is it such a hit right now? Or more of a business angle: how much money do we spend on Product Z each week? Or even a reader-based approach: where to get empanadas near school?

Personal stories: How someone relates to food can make a beautiful piece of writing that allows a writer to really show his or her personal voice. **This could be an essay on cooking with a favorite relative or an experience eating in another country, but whatever the subject is these personal stories should be written to be savored.** The flow and the pace of the piece should transport the reader into a space designed by the writer to be unique and visual.

Understanding cultures: What do Muslims eat to celebrate Eid al-Fitr, the end of Ramadan, a month-long religious holiday of fasting? How do local farmers honor the yearly harvest? **Food is a gateway to understanding people's traditions, culture, and history.** These features should educate you as the writer as much the reader. One word of caution: Be careful of writing about things you are unfamiliar with. You never want people to feel like you are highlighting them for being "weird" or "different." Remember everybody has a place in your school community and you should aim for inclusivity in your writing. Also, remember that while food can help you understand a culture, people are more than what they eat, so avoid stereotyping or using food as way to catagorize a group of students.

Profiles: Getting people talking about food is a great way to learn more about them. When it comes to writing a profile about a local restaurant owner or a teacher with a food-related side hustle, the interview should be as natural as a conversation. **Get the subject talking about their personal connection to food.** Find out how that connection has evolved over time, and how their professional interaction with food has enriched their life. Just like with all profiles, quote more than the subject as a source. Students who are customers or who have connected to the subject can provide valuable insight that make the topic relatable to your readers.

A Note on Adjectives

Writing feature stories can be a fun break from news writing, which can feel stifling at times for new writers. But that doesn't mean you can break all the rules. You still need to be efficient with your word choice and aim for specific, visual communication.

It's easy to rely on adjectives in feature writing—especially when writing about food. But be careful. Describing something as "good" or "delicious" isn't useful. Use all of your senses to describe that dining experience, whether the food is as simple as a piece of fruit or complex as a four course meal. What analogies can you create to describe the experience? Challenge yourself to write something no one has written before.

Reviews

Reviews may seem a lot easier to write than they are. Yes, as part of the assignment you get to do something fun—see a movie, go to a concert—but to convey that experience to readers requires more than telling them whether or not you had a good time. The review needs to go deeper than declaring the event a hit or miss. You need to consider the target audience. A documentary on fracking has different goals than a sci-fi thriller. Your aim is to tell the audience how well the creator achieved his vision. Let the reader know if the experience is worth their time and money.

How to Write a Valuable Review

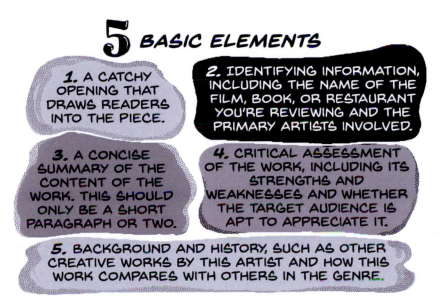

5 BASIC ELEMENTS

1. A CATCHY OPENING THAT DRAWS READERS INTO THE PIECE.

2. IDENTIFYING INFORMATION, INCLUDING THE NAME OF THE FILM, BOOK, OR RESTAURANT YOU'RE REVIEWING AND THE PRIMARY ARTISTS INVOLVED.

3. A CONCISE SUMMARY OF THE CONTENT OF THE WORK. THIS SHOULD ONLY BE A SHORT PARAGRAPH OR TWO.

4. CRITICAL ASSESSMENT OF THE WORK, INCLUDING ITS STRENGTHS AND WEAKNESSES AND WHETHER THE TARGET AUDIENCE IS APT TO APPRECIATE IT.

5. BACKGROUND AND HISTORY, SUCH AS OTHER CREATIVE WORKS BY THIS ARTIST AND HOW THIS WORK COMPARES WITH OTHERS IN THE GENRE.

- Do your research. You may refer to earlier work or life events but keep the focus on the current work.
- Always provide supporting evidence for your opinion. Here are some specific items you'll want in your reviews:

> Limit the plot synopsis in a movie or book review to a few sentences. You don't want to give away any spoilers and a review shouldn't be written as a summary of the plot. The review should focus on the craft and the execution of the work. For example, most biographies or biopics are going to have the same basic outline—someone wasn't a big deal and then she became a big deal. Your focus should be on describing how well this particular writer or team of writer/director/actors managed to produce a compelling version of this person's story.

As you become more comfortable writing reviews, you'll learn to recognize the difference

MOVIE/TV	FOOD/RESTAURANT
Who is the director/lead actors/writers? What else have they done? Any pertinent background info? Is it part of a series?How many seasons? What are the current box office sales? (movies) What else like this already exists? (TV) What makes the best scene so good? What makes the worst scene so poorly done?	Who is the chef? Who runs it? How does this place compare to others in the neighborhood? How much do individual items cost? What are the options for vegetarians? Would you bring your parents there? Would you go there on a date?
EVENT	RECORDED MUSIC
What was the focus? What were some of the highlights of it? How well was it organized? Was it easy to get to different areas? What was the crowd like? What services were provided?	Look at the album as a collection of songs and your review is an overview. Don't review each song—though you can refer to individual tracks. Consider how the album fits together as a whole and how it compares to past work.

between your liking something and something being well done. For example, even if you don't care for oatmeal cookies, you should be able to distinguish between cheaply made store bought cookies and one from your local bakery. Your opinion is a key part of the review process but your personal preferences shouldn't be.

Did you know?

The Association of Food Journalists publishes a list of guidelines on its website for food critics: https://www.afjonline.com/.

Get Ahead of the Game

What value is a review of a play that ended its run before the article was published? For many occasions, an article about an event before it goes public offers a better service to your readers. These stories are called advances or previews and give the reader a heads-up on forthcoming events. The key is to be short and lively and to include quotes and intruiging sneak preview tidbits. Give people a reason to go.

Sports Features

There is more to writing about sports than providing game coverage. That being said, a recent game can offer access to current information on everything you'd like to cover from the training schedule of student athletes to team financials.

Use these questions to help brainstorm sports features for your school publication:

- Do any of our coaches have experience on a professional team?
- What's the nutritional need for a student athlete? How do the athletes keep up with their nutritional intake?
- What team members are getting sport scholarships?
- Who pays for school sports?
- What rules in our school district pertain specifically to athletes?
- What fan has been to every single game?
- Who has siblings who excelled in the same sport in previous years?
- Who has a remarkable challenge to overcome that makes his or her involvement in the sport unique?
- What are the game-day ritual for team members?
- How have team uniforms changed over the years?
- What are athletes and/or coaches favorite sports-related movie?
- Do any athletes have religious practice that interfere with (or are complicated by) team activities?

Game Day

Sports writing is a great place to use active verbs and descriptive writing to convey the action of a game to readers. Here are some things to include in your game day stories:

- the score and who won
- names of teams involved and which school they are affiliated with
- lively details of exciting moments
- season record of your school's team
- team rivalries
- highlights or turning point plays
- quotes from coach and pivotal players
- record (or nearly) breaking statistics or plays
- how the game affects the team's standing in the season

Just remember, there's no cheering in the press box. Your tone should remain neutral. Of course you want your school's team to win, but your readers shouldn't be able to tell that. Even sports stories are reported and based in fact. You shouldn't be advocating for a team, just reporting on it.

- Any complaints of sexism, racism or homophobia within the department?
- What's in an athlete's gym bag?
- What's their favorite piece of equipment?
- What are the most common injuries in each sport?
- What player has been sidelined for injury most?
- How do players prep energy-wise for a game?

Don't limit these prompts to just sports. With a few tweaks these questions can help you brainstorm features for most other clubs at your school.

How to Write a How-To Story

Service journalism is the mainstay of magazines. The goal is to engage readers with information they can use. While some of these articles can come across as light listicles or clickbait, you want to make sure they contain reported articles—not just writer-to-student advice pieces. Reporters must talk to others and organize and summarize the information for full reader engagement.

HERE ARE SOME POTENTIAL TOPICS:

- HOW TO START A SCHOOL CLUB
- HOW TO ASK SOMEONE OUT
- HOW TO GO ON A DATE
- HOW TO GET TO SELECT THE RIGHT COLLEGE FOR YOU
- FIVE PLACES TO GO AFTER SCHOOL FOR A SNACK
- HOW TO FIND SOMETHING YOU LOST AT SCHOOL
- HOW TO REPLACE A BUS PASS/LUNCH PASS
- HOW TO MAKE THE MOST OF YOUR TIME--HOW TO GET TO BED BEFORE 2 A.M.

- HOW TO ASK A TEACHER FOR A RECOMMENDATION
- HOW TO GET A SUMMER JOB
- HOW TO GET TO SCHOOL ON TIME
- HOW TO MAKE A GOOD AND FAST BREAKFAST
- HOW TO GO IMPRESS DURING A JOB/COLLEGE INTERVIEW
- HOW TO SPEND LESS ON PROM
- HOW TO AFFORD SENIOR YEAR
- HOW TO PERSONALIZE YOUR MOBILE PHONE

Who do you interview?

What makes service journalism useful is that the information comes from someone who has knowledge in the area. So you'll need to interview a few people who have created a school club, asked someone out, or managed to get 7–8 hours of sleep a night.

When possible, you want to interview an expert, too. Like a local chef for the "How to make a good and fast breakfast" or the manager at a place that hires teens for the "How to impress during an interview" article.

Writing guidelines:

Don't worry if the articles seem formulaic. You'll have fun enough writing the piece that the reader will appreciate the clarity the formula provides.

1. Present the problem: you're always late to school
2. Set up the solution: We talked to three students who are always on time
3. Break it down into bullet points or short paragraphs and bolded section intros.

Don't forget to include:

- What NOT to do
- Visuals—photography or illustrations

The Journalistic Takeaway: Be Relevant and Responsible

Write for your readers.

It's important that a news organization reports the news of the community and investigates deep issues. But as Jasmine points out, it is equally important for student publications to show their readers that they are also part of the student body. By reporting on a trend in the dating habits of students, *The Hallway Monitor* has its pulse on the community it is covering.

The key is to have balance in your coverage. Just like a well-balanced dinner is a mixture of protein, vegetable, and grain, your coverage should be a mix of news, trends, service journalism, sports coverage, opinion, and features.

Listen to your staff.

Trixie is the editor but that doesn't mean she is right all the time. She knows this and gives Jasmine the chance to go to bat for her own section. It's important to let editors be in charge of their departments in this way. It builds leaderships skills and gives editors the ownership they need to do a good job with their sections.

This can also trickle down on the reporter level. If you're a section editor, let your reporters be in charge of a beat. The more freedom they are given to find stories the more they will be invested in the work.

Leading is not about winning and being right. It is about helping your peers become the best journalists they can be and producing a news publication that reflects the efforts of the whole staff.

Be responsible.

Many censorship arguments over controversial issues stem from administrators fearing that students may be encouraged to try questionable behaviors after reading about the topic. This is why Jasmine and Trixie made sure the dating package feature couldn't be interpreted as a "How To" guide to dating older men. It's a fine line. As a publication catering to a high school audience, you don't want to be moralistic, but you also don't want to encourage risky behavior.

The challenge before you is covering a sensitive topic in a manner that doesn't glamorize or endorse it. Again, the best approach here is balance. Consider how interviews with experts, research statistics, and teen perspective and trends come together to tell the whole story.

The Story Behind the Story: Taking a Personal Look at Race

In 2001 *The New York Times* won a Pulitzer Prize for its 15-part series, "How Race Is Lived." This mammoth reporting project involved countless reporters, photographers, editors, and other staffers. However, this wasn't a breaking news story or an international event coverage. The series looks at the personal stories of race at work, church, school, and neighborhoods. "Race relations are being defined less by political action than by daily experience," the editors wrote in the series introduction.

The impetus for the project didn't come from a press release or a high profile arrest. It came from conversations in *The New York Times* newsroom that simmered for five years. Eventually the talk came to a boiling point and the concept was broken down into assignments. The goal, according to Joseph Lelyveld, the newspaper's editor at the time, was to go beyond "the usual mosaic of dreary census, school, and income statistics, studded with pious quotations from the civil rights era of blessed memory or from academics and clergymen speaking earnestly."

In a long-form narrative style the series covered the one-on-one relationships of a mixed race Pentecostal congregation in Atlanta; the multiracial workforce at a slaughterhouse in Tar Heel, North Carolina; teen girls forced apart by stereotypes and prejudice in Maplewood, New Jersey; a friendship of two Cubans in Miami torn by race; a narcotics detail in Harlem led by a black police sergeant; the battle of two columnist to coexist in an Akron, Ohio newsroom; and an Internet start-up run by two founders, one black and one white.

Keep in mind this was before police shootings became national news and before the Black Lives Matter movement. It was before intersectionality became a buzzword and immigration was an international debate. The mainstream media wasn't talking about much about race. Even though many readers were living through these scenarios, the media didn't reflect their realities of their every day lives. This is why the series had such a big impact—it went deep but was immediately relatable.

It was also incredibly difficult to report. The conversations the reporters had with their sources over a year of reporting were hard. There were tough questions to ask and even tougher to answer. There was an "emotional nakedness" in the work, as Lelyveld wrote. These were private conversations, private thoughts, being broadcast in a public sphere. A lot of people—and this includes the reporters and photographers from *The Times*—weren't ready to have these conversations, to admit their prejudices and to process the implications.

The series was by no means a comprehensive look at race, and didn't include coverage of every race. But the editors went in with the premise that "the central conundrum of American democracy can still be found in the legacy of human slavery and the relationship between blacks and whites," according to the book *How Race is Lived in America*. They did not "find all the stories there are to tell" but they found "the stories they were able to find."

Classroom Activities

Let's Practice Descriptive Writing

Take a moment and think about an apple. What color is it? How would you describe the taste? Does it have a smell? What do you hear when you bite into it? What texture is it in your mouth? How does it feel in your hands? Tell me about the environment you are eating it in—what sounds do you hear? What does the place smell like?

With these questions in mind, have your next meal or snack. Then, in narrative form, so it reads like a story, not a collection of sentences, describe the food and the experience you had eating it.

Writing a News Brief

News comes from a variety of situations: a personal experience; an observation; a dramatic event. But news can also come from a press release. A press release is a document by a company, organization or association making an announcement. The articles that are based on press releases are called News Briefs.

1. Go to the website for your state's governor. Find the section for news updates, sometimes it is called the press room. Find a press release about something that you think is interesting. Next search the internet for a news article about the announcement mentioned in the press release. The date of the news article should be very close (but not before!) the date on the press release.

2. Underline or highlights parts of the news article that are directly from the press release.

3. Make a two column table and list the differences between the news story and the press release.

4. Write a news brief. Consulting the table, write a news brief based on a recent press release from your state or town's department of education.

Other Activities

1. Visit the website for your local news source. Pick two headlines and write a pitch for the story that you think the reporter used to sell his or her editor on the article.

2. Interview a family member about a food tradition that they grew up with. Write up the interview into a 300-word story.

3. Pick three "How to" story ideas from this chapter. List three to five people you would interview for each story.

Chapter 8:
ALL TOGETHER NOW
GROUP REPORTING

Editorial Meetings

Trixie and her staff spend a lot of time in *The Hallway Monitor*'s newsroom. When they are not working on a story, they are sitting around a table and talking school news.

But what are they actually discussing at those gatherings?

Editorial meetings—or story meetings—are held to plan content, set deadlines, improve skills and to make the staff accountable for the work they are producing together. Every staff has different rules about who has to be at the meetings (usually editors) and for whom attendance is optional (usually reporters). Like any other meeting, it is a good idea to make an agenda and set an end time. People's time is valuable and you want meetings to be concise and efficient—just like a news story.

A sample agenda:

Highlight/lowlight: Share something great that happened last week and something not so great.

Notes on last issue or last week's stories: These can be shared openly in a group, or if you are short on time, as a turn and talk. It's helpful for staffers to pinpoint their success and share their disappointments. These could be personal or tied to the newspaper.

Discuss any reader feedback or online comments: It's nice to be reminded that people are reading the work.

Department updates from individual editors: Give each editor a chance to represent and lead his/her area.

Upcoming stories: Here we get to the core of the meeting. This should be more than a brainstorming session where staffers struggle to come up with ideas. Focus on the status of ongoing stories and make sure everybody is on track for meeting deadlines.

New stories: Reporters and editors should be prepared to pitch story ideas. It's easy for a meeting to go off the rails here, so watch out for side conversations and conversation tangents.

Staff management issues: editor struggles, advice for mentoring, recruiting writers. Are there any leadership challenges staffers want to discuss with their peers?

Focus for the week: Transparency. Being a newspaper editor and reporter is a big job. By focusing on one key element each week, staffers can get a better grasp on their work. Other weeks the focus could be on staff communication, verification, truth to power, leads, etc. Anything that is journalism-related will work.

Editorial Calendar

One of the best ways to keep track of deadlines and assignments is to keep an editorial calendar. This should be something that is centrally located (like on a shared drive or in the cloud), constantly updated and referred to at every meeting. Here's an example:

ASSIGNMENT	WRITER	NEXT DEADLINE	EDITOR	SCHEDULED FOR PUBLICATION	ART	NOTES
School lunch changes	Lolinda	3/19	Alex	3/17	Photos by writer	
New Weight Room	Manny	3/18	Marco	4/2	Waiting on photo rendering from construction co.	Run w/ "Teen Recession"
Teen Recession	Tatyana	3/15	Roman	4/2	None	Run with "New Weight Room"
Empty school store	Kubble	3/18	Demi	3/22	Phoena to shoot. Status ??	
Backstage @ Musical	None / photo essay	3/12	Pheona	3/17		½ page spread
School Board Mtg.			Tess	4/2		

Angles

Just as you can take a photo from different positions, you can cover a story from different angles. Varied story angles make articles specific and interesting. They add fresh life to routine stories. Instead of writing a standard review of the spring talent show, you could produce a behind the scenes photo essay on what's happening backstage during the performance. Or you could cover it by talking to teachers who participated in their own school's talent shows. It may not be direct coverage of the event, but you are using the event as a springboard to offer a fresh perspective that may be more engaging to your readers.

Writing a story from a different angle gives the reporter a chance to do follow-up reporting on a topic. Let's say you're covering the closing of the school store. This might be the headline for the first story:

Principal Closes School Store, Students Angry

But don't stop there. Think about everyone who is affected by the closing and turn that into individual stories:

Student Employees Scramble to Fill Work Hours After Closure

Local Stores Notice Small Surge in Sales After School Store Closes

Teachers Say Students Crankier, Unprepared Since Store Closed

And think ahead to the future:

Fate of School Store Space in Limbo

If you don't have the space or time to cover a story from multiple angles, don't try to force it. Instead be selective about which angle is the most promising and don't rush through the reporting.

The Journalistic Takeaway: Be Willing to Shake Up the Status Quo

Experiment with new ways of doing things and always be willing to learn.

Because you've always done things one way, doesn't mean you can't try something different. If you're a creature of habit, this can be a hard concept to roll with. But even though doing something new can be frustrating, the opportunity for growth makes it worth the challenge in the long run. The key is to note in advance why you are making this change, put a timeline on the experiment and assess the process when it is over. Not everything you try will be a success. But you'll grow as journalists with every new thing you learn.

New ideas can come from anywhere but you'll get the most value out of attending journalism conferences and events. Most states have some sort of scholastic press association or initiative. They exist to provide you with the resources you need to do your job better. Take advantage of them.

Take in cross-departmental feedback.

Your peers have valuable insight into your work—and vice versa. Just because you're not an expert doesn't mean you can't provide suggestions or input. Your perspective is probably similar to one of your readers, so it is good to speak up. That said, many people are sensitive about their work and any feedback can seem like criticism. So provide suggestions, but do it when asked.

Remember your reader.

This might be obvious, but it is easy to forget about your reader when you're knee-deep in meeting deadlines. Journalism is a public service. Yes, it's cool to run around, ask people in power tough questions, and see your byline. But you have to keep in mind who you are doing this for: The reader.

You have a responsibility to inform and engage them. When Keitha learns how students are actually reading the paper (image, headline, caption, article), it changes the way she approached her work. This is important information for writers and editors. If you know your student body is on social media, then you better have a strong presence there. The goal isn't just for each writer to build a portfolio of clips. It's to have an impact and make a difference. Your job is to figure out how to do that best.

The Story Behind the Story:
The Maestro Concept

The Maestro Concept that Trixie uses with her staff is a method of organzing content that was developed by journalism professor Buck Ryan in the 1990s. It took off in professional and student newsrooms as a way to collaboratively produce story packages that engage readers. The launching pad for the Maestro Concept came from Poynter Institute's research that tracked people's eyes when they read an article. This understanding of how people interact with an article led to a process of news production that doesn't separate an article into different elements, but unites them into a story-telling unit.

As Trixie tells Keitha, instead of operating under the assumption that the lede is going to be the first attempt to hook the reader, consider that the reader makes a decision to stick with a story based on the main photo, then the headline, the caption, and finally the lede. So the newspaper has three chances to draw readers in before they even get to the main story.

The key elements for the team to decide on before work begins are:

- A summary of the story in fewer than 30 words
- A response to readers' thought: "I'm busy, why should I care about this particular story?"
- The top three questions that would come to a general reader's mind on the issue

Each element of your package—headline, deck (or subhead), photos, text, sidebar, infographic, etc.—should address one of these key elements in some way. Once this stage is complete, the team will report, design and illustrate a package that better suits how readers interact with news.

A version of this collaborative process is inherent in many newsrooms, especially for online stories that take advantage of immersive storytelling. These pieces use technology and design to respond and interact to the reader experience. Here a few stellar pieces to inspire you:

- "Snow Fall" by John Branch, *The New York Times*
- "Out in the Great Alone," by Brian Phillips, ESPN
- "The Philip Morris Files" by Paritosh Bansal, Aditya Kalra, Tom Lasseter, Ami Miyazaki, Duff Wilson, and Thomas Wilson, Reuters (include a fully searchable online storehouse of company documents)
- "Home to Havana" by Carrie Seidman and Elaine Litherland of *The Sarasota Herald-Tribune*
- "The Year in Push Alerts" by Andrew Kahn, Holly Allen, and Rachel Withers. *Slate* also has a behind-the-scenes look as to how the piece came together

Classroom Activities

Create an Editorial Calendar

Based on what you learned about the Maestro Concept, create a calendar that a news team could use for collaborative story packages. Remember to include deadlines and who is responsible for meeting the deadline.

Design your template to incorporates these elements:

- Story summary (<30 words)
- Why should readers care?
- Three questions that a reader would want answered
- Deadlines for art
- Deadlines for text
- Who is responsible for art?
- Goals for art? What type of images will we seek?
- Writer's name
- Design elements that will be incorporated into the story—sidebar, infographic, resource box, illustration, photos, deck, etc.
- Draft headline
- Type of main art element: photo, illustration, infographic, other
- Rough layout
- Word count

Improve the Pitch

Take a look at the pitches below. Your job is to add a few sentences to each pitch to make the story more relevant or timely for your readers. This might be a statistic, school data, a reference to pop culture, or an angle that localizes the story.

1. I want to write an article about the stigma attached to mental illness in Asian-American communities. This is a big issue especially among immigrant families. The article would include personal anecdotes from sources and statistics detailing the prevalence of mental illnesses such as depression and anxiety. I plan on interviewing three Asian teen girls and a psychologist that specializes in multicultural issues.

2. The state is building its first shelter for victims of human trafficking. Safe and Sound, an organization that assists female survivors of domestic violence and commercial sexual exploitation, recently announced that shelter was the most important issue facing these victims, especially those in their teens. Interviews could be with the trafficking expert at Safe and Sound and with the leader of the new shelter.

3. Teen female athletes are five times more likely to tear their ACL—anterior cruciate ligament—than teen male athletes are.

Another Angle

Let's say your paper decided to cover the increasing rates of anxiety in teens.

1. You talked to students, a guidance counselor, a national mental health line, a pharmaceutical company and an author on the topic. List as many angles that you can think of that provide different ways of addressing the issue from interesting perspectives.

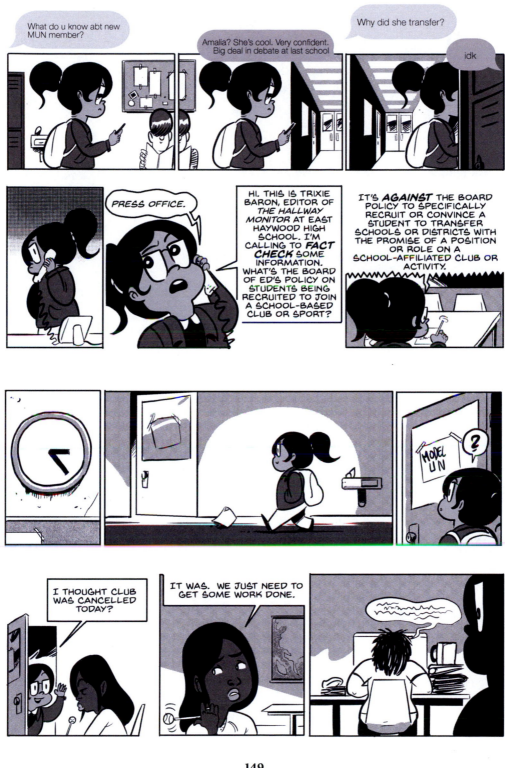

Student Journalism in the Courts

There are three main court cases that affect how freely student journalists can do their jobs.

Tinker v. Des Moines Independent Community School District

In 1969, the Supreme Court ruled that students do not "shed their constitutional rights to freedom of speech or expression at the schoolhouse gate." This decision was celebrated by scholastic journalism advocates but did not outlaw censorship.

Under Tinker, school officials can censor school-sponsored content if it's publication:

1. Will result in a material and substantial disruption of school activities
2. Invades the rights of other students
3. Falls into another area of unprotected speech, such as copyright infringement.

How do you know if your publication is school-sponsored?

Does the publication get its name, any of resources (space, technology, guidance), financial support from the school? If yes, it is school-sponsored.

Hazelwood School District v. Kuhlmeier

In a shift of law, the Supreme Court ruled in 1988 that additional factors can decide censorship in scholastic journalism, thus restricting First Amendment rights for some student journalists.

The decision focused on the distinction between student publications that were a limited "public forum" for student expression and those that weren't. The distinction between these two categories is murky and wasn't defined by the courts. However, legal experts have found that, in Hazelwood and in later decisions (see Dean v. Utica below), the main deciding factors are:

1. Are student editors driving the content decisions?
2. Does the publication operate as a public forum for student expression?

If the answer is "yes" to both of these questions, then the publication is in a stronger position to fight administrative control. Constitutionally the courts have decided that if the adviser isn't making the majority of editorial decisions and the publication identifies as a public forum, then administrators have much less authority over the publication. This is regardless of whether the work is produced as part of a school-based class or afterschool extracurricular activity.

However, if the answer is "no," school officials are allowed to censor, but only for "valid educational purposes." Again, the Court didn't define what this meant, but it did provide examples of what could be banned, including

- Content that is "ungrammatical, poorly written, inadequately researched, biased or prejudiced, vulgar or profane, or unsuitable for immature audiences."
- Sensitive topics, such as "the particulars of teenage sexual activity in a high school setting."
- "Speech that might reasonably be perceived to advocate drug or alcohol use, irresponsible sex, or conduct otherwise inconsistent with the 'shared values of a civilized social order.'"
- Material that would "associate the school with anything other than neutrality on matters of political controversy."

These examples provide a minefield of "what's okay/what's not" for student journalists. But remember, these are only for publications where students do *not* make a majority editorial content decisions and are *not* established as public forums for student expression.

It's important to note, as the Student Press Law Center does, that "Public school officials—no matter what they may say or think—do not have an unlimited license to censor." The claim that an article or image "makes the school look bad" is not a constitutionally protected defense of censorship.

Dean v. Utica Community Schools

In 2004, a federal district court in Michigan set a precedent that put some power back in the hands of student journalists. The judge determined student journalists "must be allowed to publish viewpoints contrary to those of state authorities without intervention or censorship by the authorities themselves."

The decision rested on establishing student publications as a public forum based on the paper's history in school. It also created a defense of good, quality journalism being a defense against censorship—and this applies whether or not a publication has evidence of being a nonpublic forum or a public forum. As one of the few cases brought to the courts after the Hazelwood decision, Dean provides an important road map for student journalism.

Currently there is a state-by-state movement to give student journalists more independence. The effort, called New Voices, relies on ground-level support to pass bills through state legislatures that make it harder for administrators to censor journalistic speech in a school setting. New Voices is a project of the Student Press Law Center.

Exemptions:

- Non-school sponsored student media—material produced off-site and without any school involvement—are fully protected by the First Amendment.
- Private schools operate under different rules since they are not government entities. Students should familiarize themselves with their schools' policies.

Dear Mr. Felix—I'm writing to confirm some information re: Amalia Caris' transfer to EHHS from WHS for an upcoming article in *The Hallway Monitor*. She told me that you promised her mother that Amalia would be co-captain of the Model UN club if she transferred here from Weston. Dr. Kolinski confirmed the matter was under review. How do you respond to the allegations?

Ethics

Whether you're 15 or 51, editors and reporters have to make a lot of decisions that have ethical implications for themselves, their publication and, their readers.

Here are some situations to consider:

Situation	*What to consider*
A beloved music teacher dies. You go to her home and a neighbor is there feeding her pet hedgehog. She lets you in and you find the home messy and unhygienic. You write a profile of the music teacher describes the scene at the house and focuses on how she gave her students so much attention that she ignored her own well-being.	While you can't **libel** the dead, the article may have needlessly upset the grieving family by damaging her reputation. There are questions here about whether there was an **invasion of privacy**. You didn't have a family's permission to be on property. True, your job is to report the truth, but you have to be aware of making assumptions and hurting innocent people along the way.
As the photo editor, you are looking for a picture to go along with story about teens who have a lot of credit card debt. You found a good photo online of a girl with a lot of shopping bags or you could use one you took a few months ago of a student displaying all her credit cards like a fan near her face.	If you grab an image offline you must make sure it has a Creative Commons license before you use it or you're risk for **copyright infringement** (see Chapter 5 for more information). To avoid this, you might want to use a photo you know you own. But what happens when this girl sees the photo of herself over the headline "Teens in Debt Need Parent Bailout"? The article implies she is one of the students in debt—and this is **misrepresentation**. It also might be an **invasion of privacy** if her credit card numbers can be read.
A student at your school won a national photography competition. The winning image shows way more skin than your dress code allows. Do you publish the image?	There is balance you have to strike here between **obscenity** and **artistic expression**. While the image may be nothing the student body hasn't seen before, you know it will attract the attention of administration. Are you willing to have this **censorship** battle or will you censor your publication instead?

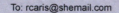

To: rcaris@shemail.com

Subject: Amalia´s transfer

Dear Ms. Caris—I'm writing an article for *The Hallway Monitor*, the student newspaper at East Haywood High school, about your daughter's transfer to EHHS. She told me today that the Model UN adviser Mr. Felix told you that Amalia could be co-captain of the club if she transferred here from Weston High School. Do you remember what Mr. Felix said to you exactly? How many times did you and Mr Felix speak about Amalia's transfer?

Max—Save me room for 400 words cover story. I'll have it to you in a few hrs. Tx.

Teacher Under Review for Model United Nations Student Transfer
by Trixie Baron

History teacher Mr. Felix is under administrative review for allegations....

What Does Censorship Look Like?

If plagiarism and fabrication are the worst crimes a journalist can commit, being censored is the worst thing that can happen to a student journalist. That's why Trixie is so upset when her article didn't get published. She was wronged.

What Is Censorship?

In the context of the scholastic journalism, censorship is the suppression words, images, or ideas that someone outside of the publication finds offensive, inappropriate, or inaccurate.

Prior review: "Occurs when anyone not on the publication/media staff requires that he or she be allowed to read, view or approve student material before distribution, airing or publication," according to the Journalism Education Association. In and of itself prior review is not censorship, but it can lead to censorship either directly or indirectly.

Prior restraint: Is an act of censorship based on an order to remove content by someone outside of the publication staff. For example, say you published a story online about the disciplinary actions the school took against underage drinkers at an off-site school-sponsored event. Hours after the story went live the principal exercised prior restraint by demanding removal of the article. Prior restraint applies to print publications if administrators make it impossible to distribute the newspaper or magazine.

Self-censorship: This is the most dangerous kind of censorship. Self-censorship is the product of administrative control that sinks into your subconscious. It starts when you find yourself not speaking up in story idea meetings or rewriting a sentence in a way that is more flattering (but less accurate) to the school or a big wig in the community. Do this enough and soon you'll train yourself not to even think of potentially controversial story topics—even if they're important.

The Journalistic Takeaway: Don't Be Rash

Be on the Defensive

Even before you have to put on boxing gloves to defend your First Amendment rights, make sure your publication is in fighting shape. Establish your publication as a public forum for student expression through policy and practice, so you have a solid foundation to counter attempts at censorship. Make sure you know the history of your publication and are familiar with any recent battles with the administration. Regularly check in with your fellow staff members to make sure you all feel like you have editorial control over the publication. And publish your "public forum" policy frequently or make it a permanent feature on the website (usually part of the "About Us" or "Contact" page).

Respond Carefully

A court case defending the First Amendment might sound exciting, but your first step in dealing with censorship is to try to do de-escalate the situation first. As team the staff has to determine if the battle is worth the fight—not all are. The determining factor isn't if you think you'll win or not, but the importance of the issue. Are you defending a minor issue (the use of an obscenity or the inclusion of a racy photo) or an important piece of journalism?

The best way to handle cases of censorship is for students to address the censor directly. Student journalists actually have more legal protections than teachers or publication advisers, who are school employees. When the students take charge of resolving these cases, they are also taking a step in asserting their rights as representatives of a public forum.

If the potential censor isn't responsive, the Student Press Law Center advises that you consider sending a press release about the censorship and consider approaching a local newspaper about publishing the censored work. You could also create an alternative (non-school sponsored) publication that allows you to serve your readers under your full First Amendment rights.

Remember, the goal here is getting the material published and getting voices heard. There are several organizations that can provide you with guidance during this process. The Student Press Law Center, American Civil Liberties Union, and Foundation for Individual Rights in Education are on your side and should be consulted when necessary.

The Story Behind the Story: The Ongoing Impact of Free Speech Court Cases

The cases that led to scholastic journalism's three biggest court rulings are as interesting as the impact of the decisions:

Tinker v. Des Moines Independent Community School District

It all started in 1965 when Mary Beth Tinker, her brother, and their friend wore black armbands to school to protest the Vietnam War. The principal had recently announced a ban on the armbands, which the school board upheld. The students refused to follow the ban and were suspended. Mary Beth was 13 at the time.

The case eventually made its way to the Supreme Court. The ruling supported free speech rights for students as long as the speech wasn't disruptive to the learning environment of the school. "They caused discussion outside of the classrooms, but no interference with work and no disorder," the Court said. This "disruption test" has been used to decide other free speech cases that draw the line against promoting drug use at school events (Morse v. Frederick) but in support of student rights to dye their hair.

Hazelwood School District v. Kuhlmeier

All Cathy Kuhlmeier, Leslie Smart, and Leanne Tippett wanted to do was publish two stories in *The Spectrum*, the newspaper they wrote and edited as part of their journalism class. The articles covered divorce and teen pregnancy. The principal deemed the topics too sensitive for younger students and refused to publish the stories. In 1988, the Court agreed with the school that the girls First Amendment rights were not being trampled on by prior review.

"Educators do not offend the First Amendment by exercising editorial control over the style and content of student speech in school-sponsored expressive activities," the Court said, "so long as their actions are reasonably related to legitimate [educational] concerns."

While the decision was clearly a setback for student journalism, it did put restrictions on what could be censored and why.

Dean v. Utica Community Schools

Fourteen years after Hazelwood was decided Katy Dean and Dan Butts, student reporters for the *Arrow* at Utica High School, found a story they couldn't ignore: a local couple had filed a lawsuit claiming the exhaust from the school bus in the garage next to their house gave the husband lung cancer. They researched scientific findings on the issue, talked to the couple, and approached the school district for a response. The article reflected officials' "no comment" response. The principal told the *Arrow*'s adviser to pull the story. School officials, including the superintendent, defended the actions on the grounds that the story was inaccurate and based on unreliable sources. The paper went to press without the article but in its place was an editorial against censorship and a black box with the word "Censored" stamped on it.

Public support was on the side of the students and a local newspaper ran the article. In 2004, Judge Arthur Tarnow called the school's censorship "indefensible." He said there was not a "significant disparity in quality between Dean's article in the *Arrow* and the similar articles in 'professional' newspapers." This 2004 case set a precedent that supported good quality journalism in the face of administrative control.

Classroom Activities

An Exploration of Ethics

For each of the three cases below, write an essay about how you would handle the situation. Consider that each case has at least two ethical considerations from this list:

- Breaking the law
- Safety of reporter
- Invasion of privacy
- Well-being of community members

- Deception
- Burning a source
- Personal responsibility
- Misrepresentation

1. Your sports photographer took an amazing close up action shot of swim team captain winning his division. The problem is the photo highlights the student's back acne. The layout editor suggests photoshopping his skin clear.

2. You're getting ready to publish a story about a Muslim student's decision to wear the hijab. One source says she wears it at home but takes it off when she gets to school. She knew she was on the record but sends you an email asking you to remove her quote because her parents might find out about it and she doesn't want to disrespect her family.

3. Your reporter wants to do a feature about how easy it is for teens to use tanning salons, even though your state laws prohibit anyone under 18 from indoor tanning. He said he'll just tell them he is over 18, if they ask.

Exercises

1. If your publication doesn't have a written statement about its position on being a public forum of student expression, write one. Make sure to be clear on who is making the editorial decisions for the publication and be specific about the wording by including the phrase "public forum of student student expression."

2. Interview ten people you know about the five freedoms of the First Amendment. Ask them to name them and then talk about the one they feel they exercise most often.

3. Write an article about the history of your publication. By tracking down previous advisers and editors, you might be able to establish the newspaper's history as a public forum, including coverage of battles it lost and won over the years. Write about the status of your state's First Amendment laws as it applies to student journalists. Consider working with a team of other students (at your paper or at another school) for this assignment.

The History of Journalism Timeline

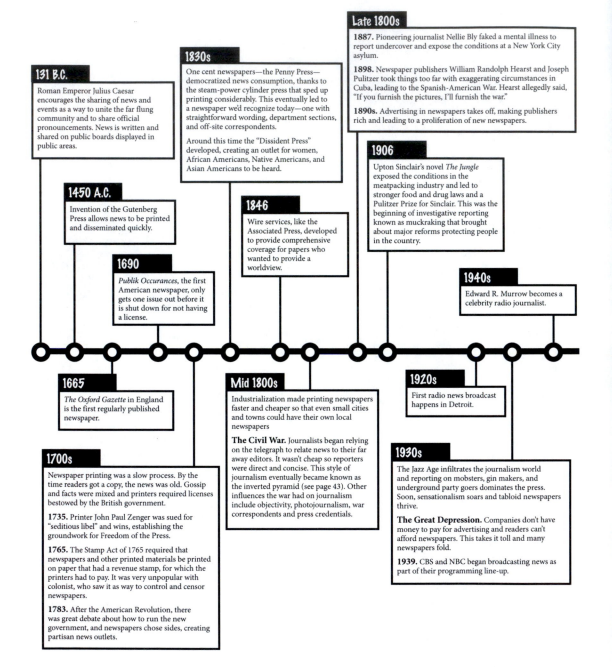

Late 1800s

1887. Pioneering journalist Nellie Bly faked a mental illness to report undercover and expose the conditions at a New York City asylum.

1898. Newspaper publishers William Randolph Hearst and Joseph Pulitzer took things too far with exaggerating circumstances in Cuba, leading to the Spanish-American War. Hearst allegedly said, "If you furnish the pictures, I'll furnish the war."

1890s. Advertising in newspapers takes off, making publishers rich and leading to a proliferation of new newspapers.

1830s

One cent newspapers—the Penny Press—democratized news consumption, thanks to the steam-power cylinder press that sped up printing considerably. This eventually led to a newspaper we'd recognize today—one with straightforward wording, department sections, and off-site correspondents.

Around this time the "Dissident Press" developed, creating an outlet for women, African Americans, Native Americans, and Asian Americans to be heard.

131 B.C.

Roman Emperor Julius Caesar encourages the sharing of news and events as a way to unite the far flung community and to share official pronouncements. News is written and shared on public boards displayed in public areas.

1906

Upton Sinclair's novel *The Jungle* exposed the conditions in the meatpacking industry and led to stronger food and drug laws and a Pulitzer Prize for Sinclair. This was the beginning of investigative reporting known as muckraking that brought about major reforms protecting people in the country.

1450 A.C.

Invention of the Gutenberg Press allows news to be printed and disseminated quickly.

1846

Wire services, like the Associated Press, developed to provide comprehensive coverage for papers who wanted to provide a worldview.

1690

Publik Occurances, the first American newspaper, only gets one issue out before it is shut down for not having a license.

1940s

Edward R. Murrow becomes a celebrity radio journalist.

1665

The Oxford Gazette in England is the first regularly published newspaper.

Mid 1800s

Industrialization made printing newspapers faster and cheaper so that even small cities and towns could have their own local newspapers

The Civil War. Journalists began relying on the telegraph to relate news to their far away editors. It wasn't cheap so reporters were direct and concise. This style of journalism eventually became known as the inverted pyramid (see page 43). Other influences the war had on journalism include objectivity, photojournalism, war correspondents and press credentials.

1920s

First radio news broadcast happens in Detroit.

1700s

Newspaper printing was a slow process. By the time readers got a copy, the news was old. Gossip and facts were mixed and printers required licenses bestowed by the British government.

1735. Printer John Paul Zenger was sued for "seditious libel" and wins, establishing the groundwork for Freedom of the Press.

1765. The Stamp Act of 1765 required that newspapers and other printed materials be printed on paper that had a revenue stamp, for which the printers had to pay. It was very unpopular with colonist, who saw it as way to control and censor newspapers.

1783. After the American Revolution, there was great debate about how to run the new government, and newspapers chose sides, creating partisan news outlets.

1930s

The Jazz Age infiltrates the journalism world and reporting on mobsters, gin makers, and underground party goers dominates the press. Soon, sensationalism soars and tabloid newspapers thrive.

The Great Depression. Companies don't have money to pay for advertising and readers can't afford newspapers. This takes it toll and many newspapers fold.

1939. CBS and NBC began broadcasting news as part of their programming line-up.

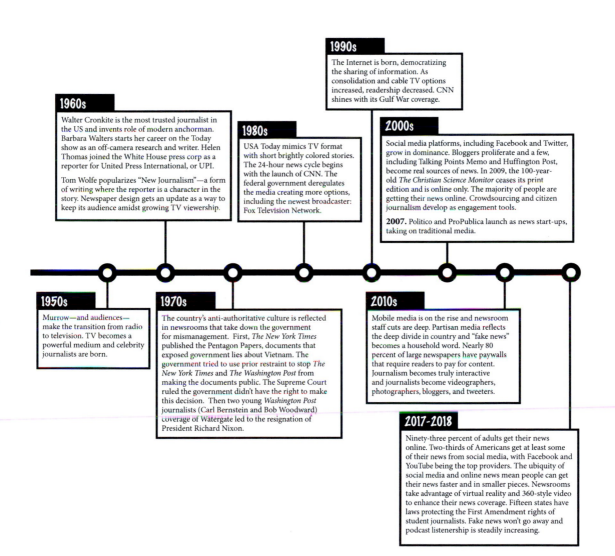

1990s

The Internet is born, democratizing the sharing of information. As consolidation and cable TV options increased, readership decreased. CNN shines with its Gulf War coverage.

1960s

Walter Cronkite is the most trusted journalist in the US and invents role of modern anchorman. Barbara Walters starts her career on the Today show as an off-camera research and writer. Helen Thomas joined the White House press corp as a reporter for United Press International, or UPI.

Tom Wolfe popularizes "New Journalism"—a form of writing where the reporter is a character in the story. Newspaper design gets an update as a way to keep its audience amidst growing TV viewership.

1980s

USA Today mimics TV format with short brightly colored stories. The 24-hour news cycle begins with the launch of CNN. The federal government deregulates the media creating more options, including the newest broadcaster: Fox Television Network.

2000s

Social media platforms, including Facebook and Twitter, grow in dominance. Bloggers proliferate and a few, including Talking Points Memo and Huffington Post, become real sources of news. In 2009, the 100-year-old *The Christian Science Monitor* ceases its print edition and is online only. The majority of people are getting their news online. Crowdsourcing and citizen journalism develop as engagement tools.

2007. Politico and ProPublica launch as news start-ups, taking on traditional media.

1950s

Murrow—and audiences—make the transition from radio to television. TV becomes a powerful medium and celebrity journalists are born.

1970s

The country's anti-authoritative culture is reflected in newsrooms that take down the government for mismanagement. First, *The New York Times* published the Pentagon Papers, documents that exposed government lies about Vietnam. The government tried to use prior restraint to stop *The New York Times* and *The Washington Post* from making the documents public. The Supreme Court ruled the government didn't have the right to make this decision. Then two young *Washington Post* journalists (Carl Bernstein and Bob Woodward) coverage of Watergate led to the resignation of President Richard Nixon.

2010s

Mobile media is on the rise and newsroom staff cuts are deep. Partisan media reflects the deep divide in country and "fake news" becomes a household word. Nearly 80 percent of large newspapers have paywalls that require readers to pay for content. Journalism becomes truly interactive and journalists become videographers, photographers, bloggers, and tweeters.

2017-2018

Ninety-three percent of adults get their news online. Two-thirds of Americans get at least some of their news from social media, with Facebook and YouTube being the top providers. The ubiquity of social media and online news mean people can get their news faster and in smaller pieces. Newsrooms take advantage of virtual reality and 360-style video to enhance their news coverage. Fifteen states have laws protecting the First Amendment rights of student journalists. Fake news won't go away and podcast listenership is steadily increasing.

Fake News: Knowingly false information delivered as fact and disguised as news, intending to mislead, disrupt and discredit the news media.

Headlines

If a nut graf is a story in a nutshell, the headline is the story at a glance.

You basically have 5–9 words to sum up your entire story. This is the Olympics of tight writing. Like the lede, the headline helps you catch your reader. The goal is to be direct, clear, and, above all, accurate. A headline should be easy to read and straightforward.

Sample Headlines

Search Dog Needs Public's Help For Vital Operation
Chamber Seeks Applications For Woman Of The Year
Environmentalists Sue To Block Refuge Road
Private Colleges Fight Waning Enrollment
Administrators Begin 'Challenging' Budget Process
Internalized Ableism Disables Some Teen Girls
Trump Presidency Pushes Some International Students To Rethink U.S. Colleges
Students Sometimes Face 'Lunch Shaming' When They Can't Pay
Tougher Reading Test Means More Students Could Be Held Back
Volunteers Unite To Support Library Through Marsha's Friendship
Council Supports Hawthorn Neighborhood Rental Prohibition In 3-2 Vote
Monument Reductions Threaten Future Dinosaur Discoveries

What do you see in these headlines?	What don't you see?
Subjects, verbs, nouns Energetic, alive and interesting verbs Subject and verbs are close together, so are adjectives and nouns No unnecessary words.	"Be" verbs Articles—an, a, the Passive voice Past tense Unfamiliar acronyms Sensational facts Inactive verbs, like "feels" or "thinks"

These are generally good rules to follow when writing your own headlines. Condensing 500 words into five words can be hard. Here's a trick: Pretend you have to pay your editor for every word in your headline. For every word you don't use, you save $1. Goal: Pay your editor no more than $5. One thing to look for is key words or phrases that repeat themselves in the article. What is the action towards that phrase? Who is doing that action? These questions can help you come up with a headline with a punch.

Note: When quoting a source in the headline, use single quotation marks.

If you use a short catchy headline for feature, make sure you write a secondary, more explanatory headline beneath it. Examples:

Dear Ms. Mayor:
Students Share Their Vision for the City

Choke Hold:
The Fossil Fuel Industry's Fight Against Climate Policy, Science and Clean Energy

Building for the Future:
Francis Lewis Hosts Robotics Competition

Word Play

It may be tempting to show off how clever you are in a headline but like everything else there is a time and place for word play. Puns are not appropriate on serious stories where people are hurt or scared. Make sure the tone of the headline matches the tone of the article. Sometimes unintentional world play sneaks in to headlines. Example:

- Man Accused of Killing Lawyer Receives a New Attorney
- Blind Girl Gets New Kidney from Dad She Hasn't Seen in Years
- Enraged Cow Injures Farmer with Ax
- Farmer Bill Dies in House
- Iraqi Head Seeks Arms
- Juvenile Court Tries Shooting Defendant
- Lung Cancer in Women Mushrooms
- Nicaragua Sets Goal to Wipe Out Literacy

Be especially careful of nouns that may come across as verbs and vice versa.

Online Headlines

Some stories have different headlines in print than they do online. There are a number of reasons why this happens:

- One version has updated information that alters the headline
- The design of print headline require different word choice
- The online headline is designed for search engine optimization (SEO)

If your goal is to have a national and international audience, you may consider tweaking your headlines in a way that makes it more likely that they show up in internet searches. The idea here is to use keywords that a reader might use when doing research.

Example

Blaze Tears Through Mott Haven Building (print)
Fire Destroys Mott Haven Building (online)

In an online search the average person is more likely to use the word "fire" than "blaze" when looking for information.

Other things to keep in mind for online headlines:

- Last names are sufficient in print headlines, but use the full name online since that is what people traditionally use when searching.

- Place names in headlines are useful for attracting readers

Just remember, online headlines need to follow all the other rules of headline writing. It needs to be logical, readable and accurate.

Covering Events and Speeches

Coverage of events and speeches is easy to pitch to editors. They like for reporters to be engaged in the community and the stories are self-contained—all the the relevant players, the best sources for information, are gathered together in one place. But that doesn't mean the coverage is easy to write. A rookie mistake when covering an event or speech is leading with the fact that it took place:

Events

"The robotics club held its annual competition on Tuesday afternoon in lunch room. Thirty-four students participated and had a blast."

"Famous author Celina D'Leon spoke to Mr. Rosenberg's 10th grade English class last month about her new book, *Philly Bird*."

Everything in these ledes is factual, but they lack vibrancy. They also lack news. What was the news of the robotics competition?

Maybe it was:

"Freshman Amanda Shannon stole the gold at last week's robotics competition. Her self-designed robot impressed judges with backflips and 90 degree turns."

Or this:

"The trend of gymnastic robots bowled over the judges at last week's competition. Compared to last year's robots, who had trouble moving forward at a consistent pace, this year's contenders flipped, turned and danced in time to music."

Speeches

Look for the news. When you're covering a guest speaker, the news might be a little harder to track down. Look for a theme that linked the speaker's remarks to the school or how the talk is relevant to students lives. For example:

> "Celina D'Leon studied for the SAT in between concessions stand customers at the movie theater where she worked during high school. Twenty years later the author of award-winning "Philly Bird" still likes to work in short bursts."

Or

> "Before she took the final question of the period, author Celina D'Leon stood up from her seat in the front of the classroom, grabbed a marker from Mr. Rosenberg's desk, and wrote her email address on whiteboard. "If you won't forget me, I won't forget you," D'Leon, author of the award-winning *Philly Bird* said to the class. D'Leon, whose novel focuses on softball-playing snowy owls, talked a lot about her memories of being a young writer in her visit to the 10th grade history class.

These articles should not read as transcripts of the event. Journalists have to use their judgement as reporters and writers to making the event relatable and interesting.

Event Coverage Reminders:
- Don't automatically write the piece in chronological order.
- Lead with the **news** of the event. The news of the event is not that the event took place but what happened or what was said at the event that was newsworthy.
- Keep it third-person and interview audience members if appropriate.
- Include how many people were there and where it was held, but not necessarily in the lede.

Let's say you're an editor and you assigned two reporters to cover the Haywood High Hoedown. They came back with the following two stories. Which would you publish? Why?

Hoedown Honors Local Farmers *by Frankie Lopez*	**Hoedown Honors Local Farmers** *by Frankie Lopez*
Two weekends ago on Saturday night the Haywood High Hoedown was held to honor area farmers. It was organized by Willie Prost, president of the school's Young Farmers of America afterschool club. He is a junior. Prost welcomed the crowd telling everyone the event was "a gift to those who had paved the way." The ball, he said, was also an effort to spotlight an issue rarely discussed: "Farmers' jobs are hard and no one knows where their food comes from anymore." After the speech, a band played many songs that people danced to. Those that didn't dance, enjoyed the pot luck supper supplied by area families. Hundreds of people attended. On the way out, people were encouraged to take information with them about farm tours, healthy eating, and local farmers markets. "Sounds good!" said Matt Berning. He picked up a recipe for green bean and steak salad. The event lasted until 10 p.m. but the awareness raised will last a long time, Prost said. "These guys needed this," he said. "And the community needed to know their struggles." Many older farmers have had a hard time lately. It's hard for them to make ends meet. Between government regulations, the expense of organic farming and the rise of fast food restaurants, Alpine has 37 percent fewer farmers than it did five years ago, according to county records released last month.	As hundreds of participants ascended the hay-strew staircase at Alpine's Town Hall, junior Willie Prost dashed around the foyer—embracing a student who arrived in a cow mask; bumping fists with a stooped, tuxedoed gentleman; and occasionally sending a "Yee-Haw!" across the room. He fanned himself aggressively. He was doing it all in six-inch spurs. The soiree, held one Saturday evening in October, was the inaugural Haywood High Hoedown, an event intended to honor area farmers and dreamed up by Prost. Guests arrived from across the county. Some came dressed in their work overalls and sun-protection gear, and others had spiffed up for the occasion in a clean button-down shirt tucked into their good jeans. The ball came at an important moment for farmers in Alpine. Last month the county announced that there were 37 percent fewer farmers here compared to five years ago. Prost, president of the school's Young Farmers of America afterschool club, said the event was "a gift to those who had paved the way" for those who want work the land professionally. The ball, he said, was also an effort to spotlight an issue rarely discussed: "Farmers jobs are hard and no one knows where their food comes from anymore." To make sure participants remembered the goal of the evening, brochures on farm tours, recipes for quick and healthy meals, and a calendar of local farmers markets filled a table near the coat check. On his way out, football quarterback Matt Berning picked up a recipe card for green bean and steak salad. "Sounds good!" he said, slipping the card into his backpack.

171

"Be" Verbs

A sure way to write more compelling content is to use active verbs instead of "Be" verbs. "Be" verbs include: Is, Am, Are, Was, Were, Be, Being, Been

Examples

Remove the "be" verb:

✗ While Riot Grrrls self-produced zines with explicitly "anti-establishment" themes, today's **teens are creating** content for mainstream audiences.

✓ While Riot Grrrls self-produced zines with explicitly "anti-establishment" themes, today's **teen create** content for mainstream audiences.

✗ These girls **are participating** in the department's self-defense class for young women.

✓ These girls **participated** in the department's self-defense class for young women.

Replace the "be" verb:

✗ Michael B. Jordan **is** the star of *Creed*.

✓ Michael B. Jordan **stars** in *Creed*.

Fewer words and active verbs—a win-win!

Change the subject:

✗ **There were** some tasty recipes in that cookbook.

✓ This **cookbook produced** some tasty recipes.

✗ After lunch, **there was a band** that played.

✓ After lunch, **the band played**.

By changing the subject of the sentence and rearranging the order of the words, the sentence becomes more direct and clear.

Combine sentences:

✗ Bea **Mushkat was disturbed** by her school's lack of response to these incidents. So she mobilized 40 students at Union High School in a walkout on November 11 and later met with area teens who had had similar experiences. **That was the beginning** of Students Against Haters.

✓ Bea **Mushkat, disturbed by** her school's lack of response to these incidents, mobilized 40 Union High School students in a walkout last year. Later she met with area teens who bonded over similar experiences and together **they launched Students Against Haters**.

Thanks to Pennington Publishing (http://blog.penningtonpublishing.com) for inspiring and informing this section.

"BE" VERBS

IS AM WAS Were be Being BEEN

TO ELIMINATE "BE" VERBS

SEARCH
CIRCLE OR HIGHLIGHT "BE" VERBS.

REMOVE
CHANGE ENDING OF THE REMAINING WORD TO FIT WITH THE SENTENCE.

REPLACE
USE AN ACTION VERB.

CHANGE
THE SENTENCE SUBJECT AND REARRANGE THE WORDS USING AN ACTION VERB.

COMBINE
THE SENTENCE WITH ANOTHER ONE TO ELIMINATE THE "BE" VERB.

Incorporating Sources

Attribution, Transitions, and Set-ups

Quotes dully layered between a lede and a kicker with some background or research slapped in like mayo. Does this sound familiar? Yup, it's a quote sandwich. It's a fast way to meet your deadline but it's not very satisfying. While news and feature writing may feel formulaic at first, the craft of writing—the fun part really—is figuring out how to fit all the pieces together in one smooth narrative.

Let's take a moment to look at the attribution, transitions, and set-up that connect the source-related elements of your story.

Attribution

An attribution tells the reader where the information in your story comes from. Whether it is a quote, a concept, a statistic, or a research finding, your job is prove to the reader (and your editor) that this material did not come from your head, but is rooted in the real word. Attribution provides proof that your information is verified.

And while attribution is necessary, it's not always interesting.

Compare the following two examples:

✗ Dr. Depthia Oswald, the Nellie Bly Chair of Parenthetical Studies at Paraskavas Center in Sarasota, Florida, said, "Dating can be a gold mine or a landmine for teens with disabilities."

✓ "Dating can be a gold mine or a landmine for teens with disabilities," said Dr. Depthia Oswald, the Nellie Bly Chair of Parenthetical Studies at Paraskavas Center in Sarasota, Florida.

In the first example, the reader gets lost in the wordiness of the attribution and the power of the information loses its punch. Put the attribution after the interesting research finding, not before it. You don't want to trap the reader in a jumble of university names and affiliations.

Set-Ups as Transitions

Before you bring a new source into an article, you want to figure out what part of the story that source represents. How does her input add on to what the previous source said or experienced? Why do you want the reader to hear from this person? If it is just that she agreed with the previous source, then don't use the quote, or figure out a way to distinguish it from the previous one.

If everyone in your story is saying the exact same thing, then you haven't done enough reporting. You also don't want everyone in your article to be talking about wildly different topics that have no connection. Your job is to choose quotes that are on the same topic but have nuanced differences that support your nut graf.

Once you determine a source's role in your story, use that information to set up their quotes or their segment of the article. This set-up tells the reader what the source has to offer to the conversation.

Shannon Berkeley, 37, had something interesting to say on the topic.	◄— **This is generic and doesn't tell the reader Berkeley's role in the story. Also, "interesting" is subjective.**
Berkeley, the CEO of Fabulous Beans, a button manufacturer, said, "I was going through a corporate merger when I found this place. Maybe it's the air or the ocean views. It just felt like a peaceful place for me." She now lives in a former synagogue on the South Shore.	◄— **It take the writer too long to get to what Berkeley says. Remember readers like quote but they aren't willing to bush-whack through a set-up to get there.** **A three sentence quote is pretty long to read all at once.**
When Shannon Berkeley, 37, moved into the former synagogue on the South Shore, she didn't realize that her new home would be a healing place for her.	◄— **This is specific and tells the reader Berkeley's role in the article, distinguishing her from other sources.**
"I was going through a corporate merger when I found this place," said Berkeley, the CEO of Fabulous Beans, a button manufacturer. "Maybe it's the air or the ocean views. It just felt like a peaceful place for me."	◄— **At this point readers are hungry for a quote and the writer gives them one.** ◄— **Interrupting a quote, like this, is a great way to sneak in the attribution in while the reader is eager to hear more from the source.** **Notice how the and where the quote is interrupted. One sentence up front and two in the back. The first makes you want to more and then the others complete the thought and tie into the set-up.**

The second example doesn't begin with the person's name or lead with the attribution, which demonstrates how you can highlight the relevence of a new source for the reader. It's like introducing two people at a party. You say why you think they might be friends, not just their name and affiliation.

Don't write "when asked" in an article. Instead white the response as a transition to the next quote:

Example: When asked how she learned about the festival, Smith said, "I was born and raised in Trinidad and Tobago, and event though I am Christian my dad's side of the family is Hindu. To show respect to my grandmother, my sister and I would respect the traditions and take part in celebrating with her."

Rewrite: Smith, who grew up in Trinidad and Tobago, said she learned about the festival from her father's side of the family, who is Hindu. "To show respect to my grandmother, my sister and I would respect the traditions and take part in celebrating with her."

Use of Sources: A Checklist for Reporters & Editors
For News and Feature Stories
Used with permission from the NYC High School Journalism Collaborative at Baruch College

Headline of article reviewed:_____

Reviewer: _____

Uses an Objective, Third Person Perspective	*Yes*	*No*	*N/A*
Are any of these words used in the news or feature article, with the exception of quoted material: I, you, me, we, us, our, your, etc.?	☐	☐	☐
Are any words capitalized, italicized, or in quotation marks that are not part of quoted material?	☐	☐	☐
Are exclamation points used outside of quoted material?	☐	☐	☐
Do any words reveal how the writer feels about the topic?	☐	☐	☐
Are individual sources referred to as "him," "her," "she," "he," or "it" (not "they" or "them," unless a source prefers a plural pronoun).	☐	☐	☐
Does the writer avoid cheerleading for the school?	☐	☐	☐
Provides Multiple Independent Sources and Is Fair			
Are there at least four sources used in the article (at least two for profiles)?	☐	☐	☐
Does the article contain at least three quotations from different sources?	☐	☐	☐
Are a variety of viewpoints represented, including all major perspectives?	☐	☐	☐
Does the article quote students from a diversity of perspectives, including different grades and genders?	☐	☐	☐
Did the writer avoid quoting his/her best friends or newspaper colleagues as representatives of student opinion?	☐	☐	☐
For an article on a controversial subject, does it include fair representation of opposing viewpoints?	☐	☐	☐
Were all relevant segments of the high school community (administrators, teachers, staff) given a chance to respond, especially anyone who is being criticized in some way?	☐	☐	☐
Relies on Original Reporting			
Is it clear where quotes came from (interview, press release, speech, etc.)?	☐	☐	☐
Are words/phrases like "many people," "most people," "everybody," "clearly," and "obviously," supported with research & reporting & named sources?	☐	☐	☐

(Uses an Objective, Third Person Perspective)	*Yes*	*No*	*N/A*
Are words representing numbers ("a lot," "many," etc.) quantifiable?	☐	☐	☐
Is the article substantially reported by the student journalists as opposed to repeating previously published material?	☐	☐	☐
Are all sources adequately identified with a) speaker/author names and relevant affiliations? b) newspaper/magazine names and article publication dates? c) internet site names, sponsoring organizations, and where helpful, urls?	☐ ☐ ☐	☐ ☐ ☐	☐ ☐ ☐
Does the article present information and opinions from in-school experts (e.g. science teachers on global warming; guidance counselors and health teachers on teen drinking)?	☐	☐	☐
Does the story include details that were gathered from reporter's own observations?	☐	☐	☐
If a story leads with an anecdote, is the anecdote true and attributed?	☐	☐	☐
Are questions asked by the writer that are not addressed within the article?	☐	☐	☐
Limits Anonymous Sources			
Does the writer use anonymous sources?	☐	☐	☐
If so, are the reasons spelled out in the story?	☐	☐	☐
Are anonymous sources, if used, sufficiently identified in terms of perspective?	☐	☐	☐
Provides Context and Relevance to the Readers			
Is it clear why this article is relevant to the school community-based reader?	☐	☐	☐
Is there information on the wider implications of this topic/issue provided?	☐	☐	☐
Was an independent/outside expert interviewed for the article if appropriate and accessible?	☐	☐	☐
Does story apply to more than one student?	☐	☐	☐
Provides Attribution for All Information, Opinion & Statements of Disputable Facts			
Does the writer reveal his/her own opinion, either directly or indirectly?	☐	☐	☐
Are statements of opinion presented as facts? (How can they be reworded to address this problem?)	☐	☐	☐
Are all opinions attributed?	☐	☐	☐
Do non-attributed facts come from the reporter's observation and is this clear in the story?	☐	☐	☐

(Uses an Objective, Third Person Perspective)	Yes	No	N/A
Is every quotation accompanied by a verb of attribution?	☐	☐	☐
Is "said" the most frequently used verb of attribution, with alternatives selected only to provide more precise information (e.g. "emphasized," "shouted," "admitted")?	☐	☐	☐
Statistics Are Nonpartisan (or at least divulge the vested interest of research provider)			
When results from polls or surveys are used, does the article state when, where, how, and by whom the poll was conducted?	☐	☐	☐
Does it report how many were polled?	☐	☐	☐
Does all data come from reputable sources?	☐	☐	☐
Is the self-interest of the research organization provided?	☐	☐	☐

This guide was created by Geanne Belton, Ilsa Cowen, Jere Hester, Katina Paron, Rob Schimenz, and Indrani Sen.

Online Sources for Copyright-Free Images and Music

Copyright Free Content

The internet can be a great resource for content that isn't covered by copyright, which can be reproduced for a variety of purposes.

- **Wikimedia Commons** (https://commons.wikimedia.org/wiki): Huge repository of free media
- **Creative Commons Search** (https://ccsearch.creativecommons.org/): Search many sites at once for videos, music and photos
- **Google Advanced Image Search** (https://www.google.com/advanced_image_search): use the dropdown menu to choose usage rights you need
- **Findicon** (http://findicons.com/): Large resource for avatars or small images
- **Open Clipart Library** (https://openclipart.org/): Public domain clipart
- **Morguefile** (http://www.morguefile.com/): Free stock photos
- **StockVault** (http://www.stockvault.net/): Free images from photographers around the world
- **Pexels** (https://www.pexels.com/royalty-free-images/): Free stock photos

Public Domain Sources

Images and videos created by U.S. government employees as part of their federal jobs belong to the public and aren't protected by copyright. Where you can find these:

- **White House** (https://www.whitehouse.gov/)
- **NASA** (https://www.nasa.gov/multimedia/imagegallery/index.html)
- **State Department** (https://www.flickr.com/photos/statephotos/)
- **Defense Department** (https://www.defense.gov/Photos/Photo-Gallery/)
- **National Park Service** (https://www.nps.gov/media/multimedia-search.htm)
- **FEMA** (https://www.fema.gov/media-library/assets/images)

Even if you find the a piece of media (photo, music, video, graphic) on one of the sites above, make sure you double check the usage rights for the item you want to publish.

And always give credit to the creator!

Check out JEADigitalMedia.org for a list of teacher-vetted free and legal music you can use on your website and in videos.

Know Your Rights: Copyright and Fair Use

Reprinted with permission through Creative Commons from the Student Press Law Center

Q: Can we copy and publish material that we find through an online search engine like Google Images?

A: The fact that material is available and easily copied on a website does not lessen its copyright protection. The best practice is always to get consent (and if you can't, consider creating your own alternative). You may be able to make a "fair use" of a limited amount of someone else's material, but it's always best to avoid copying material from a professional news service like the Associated Press that offers such material for sale (unless you so greatly alter the material that you transform it into a new work).

Q: Does it protect you against a copyright claim if you properly credit the artwork you are copying?

A: Not at all. Copyright is concerned with consent, not credit. Properly attributing a photo or a cartoon is ethically correct, but it is not a legal defense if the creator believes that your reuse of the work infringes his copyright.

Q: Can we use the logo of a business—like Pepsi or Facebook or Google—without getting permission?

A: Yes, in connection with a news or feature story about the company or the industry, like a story about the popularity of Facebook. But you cannot use it without permission for purely marketing purposes, such as putting the Facebook logo on your yearbook cover in hopes of selling more books.

Q: Isn't it safe to reuse only 30 seconds of a song, or only 10 percent of an article?

A: You'll hear various rules of thumb, but the Copyright Act itself contains no numerical or percentage "safe harbors." Material can safely be reused—a "fair use"—if the amount taken is limited to only what is necessary, and is used in a new-and-different way (such as a clip from a film to illustrate a movie review) that does not detract from the economic value of the original.

Q: Where can you find photos, videos and documents online that are fair game to be used without permission?

A: Start with federal government (.gov) sites like the White House, FEMA, NASA and others. Content created by federal employees in the course of their work is unprotected by copyright and can be freely reused. Also look for materials carrying the Creative Commons (CC) license, a voluntary alternative to copyright. Typically, such materials can be used in a nonprofit publication as long as proper attribution is given.

Q: Who owns the copyright in work done by student journalists?

A: Unless the work is done for a salary ("work for hire") or under a contract or an employee handbook that specifies ownership, the normal rule is that the creator owns the work. And that is true even if school equipment is used.

Using Open Records to Get Your Story

Four Information Sources Every High School Journalist Should Know
Reprinted with permission through Creative Commons from the Student Press Law Center.

(1) Lawsuit Records
- **Where to Look:** The Clerk's Office, Civil Division of your local courthouse. (Start with county or circuit court; U.S. District Court can also be worth a trip.) Most have computers allowing you to search for parties to lawsuits by name. Make sure you search not just for "Plainview High School" but also "Johnson County School District," and for the last name of your district school superintendent, whose name may come first in the lawsuit.
- **What to Ask for:** Once you know your case number(s), ask to see the "pleadings file." That'll give you the Complaint, the Answer and any motions—all of the documents that lay out the parties' positions.
- **How to Use It:** Remember that the claims made in lawsuits are just claims—don't assume they're all true; use attribution. Use pleadings to find the names of the lawyers, and interview both sides. Common types of lawsuits to look for include: employment discrimination, personal injury (slipping and falling, auto accidents), and contract/bidding disputes over school purchases.

(2) Police Records
- **Where to Look:** Find out what police zone or precinct handles your school's area. (If you are in the county rather than the city, the police agency for your area may be the Sheriff's Department.) Records are kept at the front desk or at the Public Information office (it's good to meet these people first and introduce yourself), or by the Watch Commander or Shift Commander.
- **What to Ask for:** Most police departments keep 2 types of records: (1) the daily log, which just says "theft of automobile at 322 Delaware Avenue, 11:45 pm," and (2) the incident report, which is the officer's detailed write-up of everything he saw at the crime scene. You can use the log to decide which incident reports are interesting to you, and request copies of those reports. You have a right to see them, unless revealing them would interfere with an ongoing investigation. BONUS: For statistics about crime trends in your city or state, look at the FBI's Uniform Crime Reporting system—they have an easy-to-use website at: http://www.fbi.gov/ucr/ucr.htm.
- **How to Use It:** You can quote directly from the crime report, of course, or use it for leads to interview witnesses and (if appropriate) crime victims. You can also use logs and incident reports to develop stories about crime trends—the log will tell you if there have been a string of auto thefts or drug arrests in the area of your school. Also remember that many other government agencies get involved when there is an arrest, including: (1) the District Attorney (or Solicitor), who prosecutes the case, (2) the jail, which holds those arrested until trial or until they post bond, and (3) the criminal court for your county or circuit (in the case of a high school student, normally the

Juvenile Court). All of these agencies will also generate records that you can request if you are researching a particular case. For instance, once a criminal investigation is closed, the District Attorney will have a "case file" that is a public record.

(3) "No Child Left Behind" / State Education Agencies

- **Where to Look:** Your state Department of Education will keep a wealth of statistics required under the federal "No Child Left Behind" law. Most state Departments of Education have sophisticated and easy-to-use websites. If you can't find what you want, all Departments of Education have an office of Public Information, Public Affairs or Media Relations to answer questions.

- **What to Ask for:** "No Child Left Behind" requires agencies to compile a lot of different statistical reports that give a quick overview of how each district is keeping up with national standards. Some interesting reports are the Annual Performance Report, the Adequate Yearly Progress Report, and the School District Report Card.

- **How to Use It:** These reports will give you a wide range of information that can be turned into news stories. How many kids in the school are getting reduced-price lunches, and has that number gone up now that the economy is in trouble? What percent of kids who graduate from schools in your district get into college? What percent of your teachers are rated "highly qualified" in the subject areas they teach? You'll want to interview experts about what the number mean, since statistics can sometimes be confusing or even misleading. And numbers always make for easy charts and graphics.

(4) Audit Reports

- **Where to Look:** Your county school board (or Board of Education) will have an internal auditor or a contract with an outside auditing company; either way, their reports are public records. Your state Department of Education will have its own internal auditor and/or will be audited by the State Auditor.

- **What to Ask for:** State agencies, especially State Auditors (also known as the Auditor General or the Audit Bureau) are pretty sophisticated and most of them post their audit reports online, searchable by topic. Use a search function to look for the word "school" or the name of your district—or call and ask if your district has been audited, and request a copy of the report. There are 2 types of audits. "Financial audits" report on the way agencies spend money. "Performance audits" look at the way government programs operate.

- **How to Use It:** A performance audit often exposes a breakdown in state health or safety programs that is important for your audience to know about. For example, take a look at this audit of the Missouri school bus driver safety program—it concludes that the state is not doing everything necessary to protect passengers: http://www.auditor.mo.gov/press/2008–36.pdf. That could be the beginning of a really interesting story—or series—for your media outlet. If you find an audit report like this one that has statewide scope, try to "localize" the story by talking with experts in your school and your district—maybe your local safety programs are better (or worse) than the ones audited by the state.

Remember...

- Public records are "public"—it doesn't matter that you are under 18, and it doesn't matter why you want a copy. You don't need a justification to see a government document.
- If you are told you can't see a document, make the agency give you a written explanation that cites a legal justification. It's their burden to say why you can't have something, not yours.
- Use the SPLC's Open Records Request Generator to save time and research—it's been proven to work time after time, it's free and easy, and it's available at: http://www.splc.org/foiletter.asp.

Style Guides for Inclusivity

One of the best things about being a journalist is the chance to learn about new things and to share the stories of a wide range of people, including those whose voices are often overlooked. But it can be hard to write about something you don't know much about or have much experience with, and sometimes that means inadvertently offending someone. You don't want to make someone feel bad or different or to fuel stereotypes or prejudices just because you don't know the right terminology to use.

Fortunately, there are resources available to help you with this:

National Center on Journalism and Disability at the Walter Cronkite School of Journalism and Mass Communication at the Cronkite School at Arizona State University

From "Disability Language Style Guide"

- Refer to someone as having autistic spectrum disorder only if the information is relevant to the story and if a licensed medical professional has formally diagnosed the person. Ask individuals how they prefer to be described. Many prefer to be described as autistic, while others prefer to be described as "an autistic person" or a person with autism.
- For those with total hearing loss, deaf is acceptable. For others, partial hearing loss or partially deaf is preferred. It is best to ask the person which term he or she prefers.
- Avoid "confined to a wheelchair" or "wheelchair-bound" as these terms describe a person only in relationship to a piece of equipment. The terms also are misleading, as wheelchairs can liberate people, allowing them to move about, and they are inaccurate, as people who use wheelchairs are not permanently confined in them, but transfer to sleep, sit in chairs, drive cars, etc.
- The word stuttering is preferred over stammering. Do not refer to an individual as a stutterer. Rather, use people-first language, such as "a person who stutters."

National Eating Disorders Association

From "Sharing Your Story Publically"

- Don't focus on graphic images or physical descriptions of the body at its unhealthiest point.
- Always provide a resource list.
- Don't provide 'tips' or play the numbers game. "I ate only X calories a day" or "He took as many as X laxatives at a time" can turn a well-intentioned story into 'how-to' instructions for someone to follow.

GLAAD

From the "Media Reference Guide"

- The term "gay community" should be avoided, as it does not accurately reflect the diversity of the community. Rather, LGBTQ community is preferred.
- "Avoid the offensive term "sexual preference," which is used to suggest that being gay, lesbian, or bisexual is voluntary and therefore "curable."

- Avoid identifying gay people as "homosexuals" an outdated term considered derogatory and offensive to many lesbian and gay people.
- Transgender women are not cross-dressers or drag queens. Drag queens are men, typically gay men, who dress like women for the purpose of entertainment. Be aware of the differences between transgender women, cross-dressers, and drag queens. Use the term preferred by the person. Do not use the word "transvestite" at all, unless someone specifically self-identifies that way.

Race Forward

From "Journalists Style Guide for Covering Immigration"

Offensive	Use Instead
illegal immigrant illegal alien illegals	unauthorized immigrant undocumented immigrant immigrant without papers migrant foreign national citizen
anchor babies	child of undocumented immigrants
illegal worker	undocumented worker
undocumented alien	undocumented immigrant immigrant entering without inspection Immigrant seeking status

ReportingonSuicide.org

Covering suicide carefully, even briefly, can change public misperceptions and correct myths, which can encourage those who are vulnerable or at risk to seek help.

Don't	Do
Use sensationalistic headlines (e.g., "Kurt Cobain Used Shotgun to Commit Suicide").	Use headlines to inform the audience without sensationalizing the suicide (e.g., "Kurt Cobain Dead at 27").
Describe recent suicides as "skyrocketing," or becoming "an epidemic."	Research the most recent CDC data and use nonsensational words to describe an increase in the suicide rate.
Describe a suicide as inexplicable or as happening "without warning." Many people who die by suicide exhibit warning signs.	Include information on "Warning Signs" and "What to Do" in your article, if possible.

You can find more examples and the full guides online.

Society of Professional Journalists

C(SPJ)DE *of* ETHICS

PREAMBLE

Members of the Society of Professional Journalists believe that public enlightenment is the forerunner of justice and the foundation of democracy. Ethical journalism strives to ensure the free exchange of information that is accurate, fair and thorough. An ethical journalist acts with integrity.

The Society declares these four principles as the foundation of ethical journalism and encourages their use in its practice by all people in all media.

SEEK TRUTH AND REPORT IT

Ethical journalism should be accurate and fair. Journalists should be honest and courageous in gathering, reporting and interpreting information.

Journalists should:

▶ Take responsibility for the accuracy of their work. Verify information before releasing it. Use original sources whenever possible.

▶ Remember that neither speed nor format excuses inaccuracy.

▶ Provide context. Take special care not to misrepresent or oversimplify in promoting, previewing or summarizing a story.

▶ Gather, update and correct information throughout the life of a news story.

▶ Be cautious when making promises, but keep the promises they make.

▶ Identify sources clearly. The public is entitled to as much information as possible to judge the reliability and motivations of sources.

▶ Consider sources' motives before promising anonymity. Reserve anonymity for sources who may face danger, retribution or other harm, and have information that cannot be obtained elsewhere. Explain why anonymity was granted.

▶ Diligently seek subjects of news coverage to allow them to respond to criticism or allegations of wrongdoing.

▶ Avoid undercover or other surreptitious methods of gathering information unless traditional, open methods will not yield information vital to the public.

▶ Be vigilant and courageous about holding those with power accountable. Give voice to the voiceless.

▶ Support the open and civil exchange of views, even views they find repugnant.

▶ Recognize a special obligation to serve as watchdogs over public affairs and government. Seek to ensure that the public's business is conducted in the open, and that public records are open to all.

▶ Provide access to source material when it is relevant and appropriate.

▶ Boldly tell the story of the diversity and magnitude of the human experience. Seek sources whose voices we seldom hear.

▶ Avoid stereotyping. Journalists should examine the ways their values and experiences may shape their reporting.

▶ Label advocacy and commentary.

▶ Never deliberately distort facts or context, including visual information. Clearly label illustrations and re-enactments.

▶ Never plagiarize. Always attribute.

MINIMIZE HARM

Ethical journalism treats sources, subjects, colleagues and members of the public as human beings deserving of respect.

Journalists should:

▶ Balance the public's need for information against potential harm or discomfort. Pursuit of the news is not a license for arrogance or undue intrusiveness.

▶ Show compassion for those who may be affected by news coverage. Use heightened sensitivity when dealing with juveniles, victims of sex crimes, and sources or subjects who are inexperienced or unable to give consent. Consider cultural differences in approach and treatment.

▶ Recognize that legal access to information differs from an ethical justification to publish or broadcast.

▶ Realize that private people have a greater right to control information about themselves than public figures and others who seek power, influence or attention. Weigh the consequences of publishing or broadcasting personal information.

▶ Avoid pandering to lurid curiosity, even if others do.

▶ Balance a suspect's right to a fair trial with the public's right to know. Consider the implications of identifying criminal suspects before they face legal charges.

▶ Consider the long-term implications of the extended reach and permanence of publication. Provide updated and more complete information as appropriate.

ACT INDEPENDENTLY

The highest and primary obligation of ethical journalism is to serve the public.

Journalists should:

▶ Avoid conflicts of interest, real or perceived. Disclose unavoidable conflicts.

▶ Refuse gifts, favors, fees, free travel and special treatment, and avoid political and other outside activities that may compromise integrity or impartiality, or may damage credibility.

▶ Be wary of sources offering information for favors or money; do not pay for access to news. Identify content provided by outside sources, whether paid or not.

▶ Deny favored treatment to advertisers, donors or any other special interests, and resist internal and external pressure to influence coverage.

▶ Distinguish news from advertising and shun hybrids that blur the lines between the two. Prominently label sponsored content.

BE ACCOUNTABLE AND TRANSPARENT

Ethical journalism means taking responsibility for one's work and explaining one's decisions to the public.

Journalists should:

▶ Explain ethical choices and processes to audiences. Encourage a civil dialogue with the public about journalistic practices, coverage and news content.

▶ Respond quickly to questions about accuracy, clarity and fairness.

▶ Acknowledge mistakes and correct them promptly and prominently. Explain corrections and clarifications carefully and clearly.

▶ Expose unethical conduct in journalism, including within their organizations.

▶ Abide by the same high standards they expect of others.

The SPJ Code of Ethics is a statement of abiding principles supported by additional explanations and position papers (at spj.org) that address changing journalistic practices. It is not a set of rules, rather a guide that encourages all who engage in journalism to take responsibility for the information they provide, regardless of medium. The code should be read as a whole; individual principles should not be taken out of context. It is not, nor can it be under the First Amendment, legally enforceable.

187

Internet Sources
by Chapter

Chapter 1

https://www.ap.org/about/news-values-and-principles/
telling-the-story/anonymous-sources
http://bettymingliu.com/2011/04/what-is-a-nut-graf/
https://www.washingtonpost.com/watergate/
http://www.imdb.com/title/tt0074119
https://youtu.be/MgaWPqt7V_M
http://content.time.com/time/magazine/article/0,9171,9
03727,00.html
http://www.vanityfair.com/news/politics/2005/07/deept
hroat200507
http://watergate.info/
http://www.newseum.org/2015/05/31/watergate-case-
study-deep-throat/

Chapter 2

http://www.spj.org/ethicscode.asp
http://www.pbs.org/wgbh/frontline/article/a-note-
from-frontline-espn-and-league-of-denial/
http://www.pbs.org/wgbh/frontline/film/league-of-
denial/
http://www.nytimes.com/2013/08/24/sports/football/
nfl-pressure-said-to-prompt-espn-to-quit-film-
project.html
http://www.npr.org/templates/story/story.php?
storyId=214909778

Chapter 3

http://ethics.npr.org/tag/social-media/
https://womensenews.org/2017/03/female-teens-
cosplay-for-self-expression-community/
https://www.ted.com/talks/paul_lewis_crowdsourcing_
the_news
http://www.journalism.org/2012/11/28/role-social-
media-arab-uprisings/
http://www.pewglobal.org/2012/12/12/social-network-
ing-popular-across-globe/
http://en.arij.net/materials/how-the-arab-spring-has-
transformed-journalism/
https://www.forbes.com/sites/tarunwadhwa/2013/04/
22/lessons-from-crowdsourcing-the-boston-
marathon-bombings-investigation/#218427224424
https://www.washingtonpost.com/local/dc-politics/
backpack-brothers-an-example-of-the-drawbacks-
to-internet-sleuthing/2013/04/18/8c0ea9fa-a852-
11e2-b8ad-87b8baf4531b_story.html?utm_term=.
ae4979afc128

Chapter 4

https://storytracker.solutionsjournalism.org/stories/
in-class-out-of-court-how-one-school-district-
triumphed-over-truancy
http://www.seattletimes.com/education-lab/bill-
requiring-community-truancy-boards-across-state-
is-okd/
http://datajournalismhandbook.org/1.0/en/delivering_
data_3.html
http://www.datavizcatalogue.com/
http://topics.nytimes.com/top/news/technology/se-
ries/driven_to_distraction/index.html
https://www.ncbi.nlm.nih.gov/pmc/articles/PMC400
1667/

Chapter 5

http://ajrarchive.org/Article.asp?id=3057
https://www.wsj.com/articles/the-iraq-war-and-stub-
born-myths-1428087215
http://www.nytimes.com/2004/05/30/weekinreview/
the-public-editor-weapons-of-mass-destruction-or-
mass-distraction.html?_r=0
http://www.nytimes.com/2003/04/21/world/after
effects-prohibited-weapons-illicit-arms-kept-till-
eve-war-iraqi-scientist.html
http://www.nytimes.com/2004/05/26/world/from-the-
editors-the-times-and-iraq.html
https://southwestshadow.com/featuredcontent/37981/

Chapter 6

http://www.nytimes.com/2003/05/11/national/11PAPE.
html
https://www.forbes.com/sites/michaelnoer/2014/11/12/
read-the-original-forbes-takedown-of-stephen-glass/
#14d18005683a
http://www.imdb.com/title/tt0323944/
http://www.nytimes.com/1998/06/19/us/boston-
columnist-is-ousted-for-fabricated-articles.html
http://www.transparencynow.com/globe.htm
https://www.cjr.org/the_feature/the_fabulist_who_
changed_journalism.php
http://www.nytimes.com/2006/03/03/business/media/
village-voice-suspends-editor-for-fabrications-in-
an-article.html
http://observer.com/2006/04/

Chapter 7

http://www.nytimes.com/library/national/race/
https://www.afjonline.com/food-critics-guidelines/

Chapter 8

http://www.nytimes.com/projects/2012/snow-fall/
#/?part=tunnel-creek
http://www.espn.com/espn/feature/story/_/id/9175394/
out-great-alone#section-1
http://graphics.chicagotribune.com/grace/#
https://www.reuters.com/investigates/section/pmi/
http://havana.heraldtribune.com/
https://source.opennews.org/articles/how-we-made-
year-push-alerts/
http://www.slate.com/articles/news_and_politics/politic
s/2017/11/the_year_in_push_alerts_how_breaking_
news_became_our_lives.html

Chapter 9

http://www.splc.org/article/2000/12/tinker-v-des-
moines-independent-community-school-district
http://s3.amazonaws.com/cdn.getsnworks.com/spl/pdf/
HazelwoodGuide.pdf
http://studentpress.org/nspa/dean-v-utica-faq/
http://jea.org/blog/2010/04/15/scj-priorreview/

Chapter 10

https://www.slideshare.net/cubreporters/journalism-
history
http://history.journalism.ku.edu/

https://www.americanpressinstitute.org/publications/re-
ports/digital-subscriptions/single-page/
https://onlinejournalismblog.com/2008/11/20/are-
these-the-biggest-moments-in-journalism-blogging-
history/#comments
https://www.scripps.ohiou.edu/mediahistory/mhmjour
1-1.htm
https://www.poynter.org/news/birth-inverted-pyramid-
child-technology-commerce-and-history
http://guides.lib.uw.edu/miloryan/listen
http://www.nbcuniversal.com/our-history#decade_2
http://www.weeklystandard.com/edward-r.-murrow/
article/8711
http://www.pbs.org/wnet/americanmasters/edward-r-
murrow-this-reporter/513/
http://www.pewresearch.org/fact-tank/2016/06/15/
state-of-the-news-media-2016-key-takeaways/
http://www.journalism.org/2017/09/07/news-use-
across-social-media-platforms-2017/
http://bwdisrupt.businessworld.in/article/The-Future-
of-News-Four-Digital-Media-Trends-That-Will-
Shape-Journalism-in-2017/22-05-2017-118644/
http://www.spj.org/ethicscode.asp
http://blog.penningtonpublishing.com/grammar_
mechanics/how-to-eliminate-to-be-verbs-in-writing/
http://www.splc.org/page/lettergenerator
http://www.splc.org/article/2015/10/copyright-and-
fair-use-faqs
http://ncdj.org/style-guide/
https://www.nationaleatingdisorders.org/community/
sharing-your-story-responsibly
https://www.glaad.org/reference
https://www.raceforward.org/sites/default/files/DTIW_
update_JournalistStyleGuide4.pdf
http://reportingonsuicide.org/recommendations/

Bibliography

Eisner, Will. *Graphic Storytelling and Visual Narrative: Principles and Practices from the Legendary Cartoonist.* New York: W.W. Norton, 2008.

Foke, Paula, et al. *The Associated Press Stylebook 2018: And Briefing on Media Law.* 2018.

Gladstone, Brooke, Josh Neufeld, Randy Jones, and Susann Ferris-Jones. *The Influencing Machine Brooke Gladstone on the Media.* New York: W.W. Norton, 2012.

Harrower, Tim. *Inside Reporting: A Practical Guide to the Craft of Journalism.* New York: McGraw-Hill, 2013.

Kovach, Bill, and Tom Rosenstiel. *The Elements of Journalism: What Newspeople Should Know and the Public Should Expect.* New York: Three Rivers Press, 2014.

McChesney, Robert Waterman, and John Nichols. *The Death and Life of American Journalism: The Media Revolution That Will Begin the World Again.* New York: Nation Books, 2011

Strunk, William, and E. B. White. *The Elements of Style.* New York: Macmillan, 1979.

Zinsser, William Knowlton. *On Writing Well.* New York: HarperCollins, 2006.

Index